Walleyes
and
Walleye Fishing

Walleyes and Walleye Fishing

By Joe Fellegy, Jr.

Dillon Press, Inc., Minneapolis, Minnesota 55401

Dillon Press, Inc.
Minneapolis, Minnesota 55401

International Standard Book Number: 0-87518-054-X
Library of Congress Catalog Card Number: 72-89440

Printed in the United States of America.

Library of Congress Cataloging in Publication Data

Fellegy, Joe, 1944-
    Walleyes and walleye fishing.

        Includes bibliographical references.
        1. Walleye fishing. I. Title.
SH691.W3F44   799.1'7'53   72-89440
ISBN 0-87518-054-X

Table of Contents

To my Dad,
who introduced me to walleye fishing
when I was three years old.

Introduction

This book stems from my interest in walleyes and my dedication to the challenging sport of angling for them. Yet the book's origin seems almost accidental. One autumn evening, after a week of fruitless and disappointing walleye fishing, I asked Nisswa guide Royal Karels if he had any books on walleyes. He laughed and replied, "Your fishing must really be slipping!"

But I'd never been more serious. My summer of guiding had been a great one, and I felt I could stake my future fishing on my own experience rather than on someone else's. Nevertheless, I still wanted to learn more about walleyes. With additional information about these fish I might accept my occasional disappointments with greater understanding, and the knowledge could help me with my fishing.

My desire to study walleyes led me to discover that good reliable books about them, at least for popular consumption, were nonexistent. How unfortunate, I thought, since the walleye is the most sought-after game fish in my region of the country, Minnesota, and is prized throughout its range, a range that covers much of the North American continent.

Popular outdoor magazines occasionally feature articles about walleye fishing. These articles, however, are often limited in scope by length requirements, lack of accurate knowledge, and editorial demands for "the unusual." Some of these articles are "personal experience stories," consisting more of travelogue, breakfast menus, and weather reports than of the real fishing stuff. "How-to" articles frequently present only one method of catching walleyes, always the "best" approach. The problem with much of the "how-to" material is that it is inspired by experiences on far-off "virgin" waters where uneducated walleyes seem to respond to nearly any tackle, places where fishing is hardly the challenge and the sport that most of us know. As with any sport, there *is* a characteristic flavor about walleye fishing and walleye fishermen, but it is one that seldom finds its way into print.

Scientific reports dealing with the walleye have been compiled by fisheries personnel of various state and provincial conservation departments in the United States and Canada. Spawning and migration habits have been studied, along with problems of growth and interrelationships with other fish and with environmental factors. However, most of this material is unavailable to sportsmen, and the information in these reports is often expressed in a vocabulary too technical for popular use.

The need for a book that would bring science and sport together so that walleye fishermen could learn more about their elusive quarry and how to catch him became increasingly evident to me. With that in mind, I set out to write this book. To the task I brought the experience gained from a yearly average of between a thousand and fifteen hundred hours of walleye fishing over the past fifteen years, a span that has witnessed revolutionary changes in tackle and methods. My fishing grounds lie mainly in Minnesota where the walleye is the "state fish." I guide in the open water season at Mille Lacs Lake, a large typical natural walleye lake that hosts the largest walleye sport fishery of any lake in the world, winter and summer. To say that I love the sport of walleye fishing would be an understatement.

Through Warren Scidmore and Chuck Burrows of the Fisheries Section of Minnesota's Department of Natural Resources, I gained access to investigational reports and scientific information relating to walleyes. The valuable and relevant information contained in these reports has also been incorporated in this book. I acquired a considerable wealth of material from across the American continent, including works by Eschmeyer, Forney, Maloney, Priegel, and others not mentioned in the notes.

The book has been written to inform rather than to

entertain, for the benefit of both casual fishermen and advanced students of walleyes. Part 1 is a study of the walleye and its habits; Part 2 contains solid walleye fishing instruction. To help capture the "flavor" of walleye fishing, Part 3 features interviews with walleye anglers from a variety of lake and stream backgrounds, speaking in the language they are used to. For added interest, the book also includes a Walleye Distribution Guide for the United States and Canada, compiled with the help of state and provincial fisheries personnel. The Guide includes places where walleyes occur naturally as well as those areas where walleyes have been introduced by stocking.

It is my sincere hope that *Walleyes and Walleye Fishing* will provide the reader with valuable insights and knowledge about walleyes and how to catch them. Of course, a successful walleye fisherman recognizes that he lacks many of the answers and will never possess all of them, regardless of what books he reads.

Natural Distribution Map

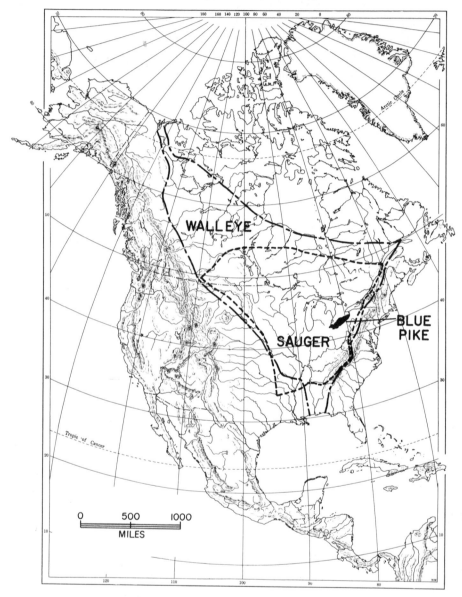

This map, provided by the Great Lakes Fishery Commission, shows the natural distribution of walleyes, blue pike, and saugers (modified from Trautman, 1957). The eastern limit of the walleye range does not include rivers flowing into the Atlantic in which the species may have been introduced, nor does the map show areas of the south and west where the walleye has been introduced.

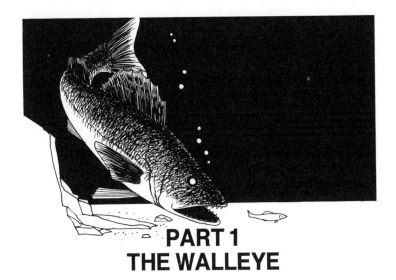

PART 1
THE WALLEYE

The walleye is a more far-ranging fish than many of us would at first believe. Walleye country covers much of the North American continent, with the Great Lakes at its center. Anglers take walleyes as far northwest as Great Slave Lake and the southernmost arm of Great Bear Lake. Some wandering walleyes have been observed at the mouth of the Mackenzie River. Walleyes range northeast to the mainland near Anticosti Island in the Gulf of St. Lawrence, and possibly into Labrador.[1] Until recently few were taken west of Nebraska at that latitude.

In the United States, the Allegheny Mountains form the eastern boundary of the natural walleye range, except for some rivers that flow into the Atlantic Ocean from Connecticut to North Carolina. The range of the sauger or sand pike, a smaller relative of the walleye, nearly coincides with the walleye's range, except that walleyes are found farther north.

Since 1940, the walleye range has widened considerably because of the creation of large reservoir lakes suitable for walleye habitation and reproduction. These new waters, along with successful stocking techniques, have brought walleye fishing to such states as Virginia, the Carolinas,

Arizona, New Mexico, Texas, Utah, and others where old "Marble Eye" had previously been a virtual unknown in angling circles.

On a map of the North American walleye range, Minnesota occupies a central position, and justly claims to be the walleye capital of the nation. Minnesota has more natural walleye lakes and offers more walleye angling than any other state. About 50 percent of the fishing water of Minnesota is considered good walleye territory, and this includes nearly all of the state's larger lakes and streams. Minnesota leads the nation in production of walleyes, with state hatcheries, rearing ponds, and winter rescue operations yielding between 150 and 200 million walleyes annually.[2] And all this is in addition to a much larger natural hatch. Many of Minnesota's large lakes are "natural" walleye producers. Their makeup is such that walleyes are able to reproduce and grow well with little or no help from state hatcheries and rearing ponds. Most of the natural walleye waters in Minnesota are in the northern half of the state.

There are basically two types of walleye lakes. First, there are the soft water walleye lakes. These lakes are at the edge of the exposed bedrock of the Canadian Shield, that massive area of granite covering much of eastern Canada and stretching as far south and west as northeastern Minnesota. Most of the Minnesota soft water lakes are in St. Louis, Lake, and Koochiching counties — lakes such as Kabetogama, Rainy, Crane, and Namakan. Soft water lakes are also scattered throughout much of Ontario. Because of their comparatively low fertility, soft water walleye lakes harbor smaller, slow-growing fish populations. Yet walleye fishing can be excellent in these lakes because of their remoteness and light fishing pressure. Moreover, yellow perch and other food fish are seldom present in large enough numbers to discourage walleyes from biting on anglers' baits.

Bedrock is exposed along the shores of these lakes. Indentations and crevices in the rocks sprout beautiful stands

Gary Noble of Border View Lodge, Baudette, Minnesota, fishes in the island country of Lake of the Woods, a walleye fisherman's paradise. Islands of granite are associated with underwater rock ledges and drop-offs, typical of the good walleye structure found in the thousands of lakes of the Canadian Shield.

of evergreens, including several varieties of pine, fir, spruce, and cedar. Islands of rock and towering pines lend majesty to these waters. In this region the watershed soils are heavy, and the richer waters have a characteristic brown stain attributed to the surrounding swamps which drain into the lakes. Here walleyes are the most important game fish, but northern pike, suckers, and tullibees abound, as do burbot, black crappies, and smallmouth bass.

Further west and south are the hard water lakes of north central Minnesota. This area is characterized by glacial out-wash sand plains and sand-gravel ground moraines along what used to be the terminal reaches of a continental ice sheet dating back thousands of years. Subsoils containing calcium carbonate or limestone have created hard water in the lakes.

Hard water lakes are usually large, often covering over one thousand acres. Their shores are sandy and have numerous gravel deposits which are ideal for walleye spawning. The wind continually stirs and aerates these shallow open waters. Within this region are such famous waters as Leech, Mille Lacs, and Winnibigoshish lakes. Along with walleyes, these lakes yield yellow perch, burbot, tullibee, suckers, northern pike, rock bass, black crappies, smallmouth and largemouth bass, and bullheads. The hard water lakes are of moderately high fertility, which en-courages faster walleye growth. Young food fish popula-tions normally reach high levels during the summer months, sometimes resulting in tough fishing. Nearly all walleye lakes, regardless of location or type, have a "clean" look about them.

It should be noted that walleyes have been stocked suc-cessfully in smaller waters, including many shallow lakes in southern Minnesota. Here walleye populations are usually maintained by stocking. The more prominent Minnesota walleye lakes and streams are discussed with some detail elsewhere in this book. Here it is sufficient to point out that Leech, Mille Lacs, Red, Winnibigoshish, Vermilion, Kabetogama, Cass, Bowstring, Lake of the Woods, Rainy, Osakis, Ottertail, and Koronis are among the most noted lakes where the walleye is popularity king.

A catalog of lake names such as this, however, is misleading because there are hundreds of walleye lakes in the Minnesota region that often rival the famous ones in walleye numbers and size. For example, personal experience has taught me that on a day when my fishing brought in a limit of two-pound walleyes from little Round Lake in Jackson County, near the Minnesota-Iowa border, I might have caught nothing at Mille Lacs or Leech. Likewise, the walleyes in Belle Lake near Hutchinson average larger than they do at Red Lake or Lake of the Woods. Thus, a balanced and non-prejudiced picture of our lake scene results in greater fishing and travel pleasures.

Walleyes are taken along most of the larger rivers, including the Mississippi, Minnesota, Blue Earth, Rainy, St. Croix, and Red Lake rivers. Smaller streams, such as the Pike River near Tower and Lake Vermilion, also offer good fishing spots.

The walleye *(Stizostedion vitreum vitreum)* is the largest member of the perch family of fishes (Percidae). While the walleye is often called a "pike" or "walleyed pike," this is a misnomer, since he does not belong to the pike family (Esocidae). Even though "walleye" is the authentic common name of this prized game fish, he is known by different names in various regions of the walleye range. For example, in Missouri he's called a "jack salmon," in Quebec he's a "doré" or "dory," and in the East he might be a "pikeperch." The long list of names used for the walleye gives ample evidence of the walleye's distribution: pike, walleyed pike, yellow walleye, jack, Susquehanna salmon, okau, white salmon, glasseye, gum pike, pickerel, and yellow pickerel.[3] The subject of this book, however, is neither pickerel, pike, nor salmon — it is a fish belonging to the perch family, whose name is simply walleye.

The blue walleye or "blue pike" is a subspecies of walleye found in Lake Erie. During the mid-1800s the blue pike became economically important to fishermen of the eastern two-thirds of that lake, where the fish inhabited the deeper and clearer waters. While the blue pike was less numerous in the shallows, especially in the western third of the lake, there appeared to be an annual movement into the shallower inshore waters and into the western part of the lake during fall and winter. Today the blue pike is considered "endangered" and faces extinction in Lake Erie.

Because coloration is particularly unstable in the walleye *(Stizostedion vitreum vitreum),* it is sometimes difficult to distinguish between the "regular" walleye, the blue pike *(Stizostedion vitreum glaucum),* and their intergrades. Sometimes the standard walleye lacks yellow and resembles the blue pike in color. In Lake Erie, "gray pike" occasionally show up in catches.

In the early 1900s the blue pike was classed as a separate species. Later, however, the blue pike was ranked as a subspecies of walleye. Physically, all body proportions of the blue pike are similar to those of other walleyes, except that the eyes of the former are larger and closer together. Dorsally, the blue pike's color is grayish blue without brassy or yellow mottlings or overcast. The sides are lighter and more silvery blue, as are the pelvic fins. The flesh of the blue pike is soft.

The blue pike of Lake Erie seldom hybridize with the sauger *(Stizostedion canadense),* although they do mingle with their larger walleye relatives to produce intergrades such as the gray pike.

The walleye is a handsome fish. He is streamlined and husky at the same time. He looks intelligent and dignified. He feels clean and presents a neat appearance. Indeed, the fact that the walleye is physically attractive when compared to many of his piscatorial neighbors is perhaps just one more reason why he is so much preferred and pursued by anglers and fish-eaters.

The walleye's body length is about six times its depth and rarely exceeds thirty inches. His width is about three-fourths of his body's depth. The walleye is covered with rough-edged scales about one-quarter inch across on wall-eyes weighing two or three pounds. The scales feel like sandpaper. There are between eighty and eighty-nine scales along the lateral line.[4]

A walleye's body is mottled, much like a perch. Each side has five irregular dark blotches, and the belly is usually white. The general color of a walleye usually varies from olive to a deep gray, flecked with gold on the sides. In the waters of the Canadian border area the walleye is more brownish. It is possible to catch walleyes of varying color tones, not only within a single state such as Minnesota, but within one lake as well. A string of twenty Mille Lacs wall-eyes might include one or two of a yellowish brown hue, which average a pound or more larger than "regular" wall-eyes and appear more chunky. They seem to fight harder, too.[5]

Walleyes have two distinctly separated dorsal fins. The first, or forward, dorsal is spiny and has narrow black margins. The membranes of the last two spines have a large black blotch at their base. The second dorsal and the anal fins are nearly opposite one another. The tissue of these fins is easily torn. Only if a hook is lodged at the base of one of these fins does the angler have a chance of fin-hooking a walleye. Occasionally "freak" walleyes, lacking one or more fins, catch the fisherman by surprise.

A walleye's tail is moderately forked, the lower tip displaying a pronounced white spot. This white tail spot, along with the black blotch at the base of the first dorsal, distinguish the walleye from the sauger or sand pike.

To the novice angler, walleyes and saugers bear a confusingly close resemblance. Saugers are generally smaller than walleyes, have a black spot at the base of each pectoral or side fin, and have rows of black spots on a spiny dorsal fin. Saugers also have large, irregular body blotches, while walleyes are more uniformly marked. In Minnesota, saugers are found mainly in the very large northern border lakes that are fed by major river systems, and in large rivers such as the lower Mississippi, lower St. Croix, and the Rainy River watershed in the Minnesota region. Lake of the Woods, Kabetogama, Namakan, Lake St. Croix, and Pepin are favorite lakes for sauger fishing. In Lake Pepin, a widening of the Mississippi River south of the Twin Cities, anglers catch twice as many saugers as they do walleyes. Saugers over two pounds are considered "fair-sized." The Minnesota sauger record is slightly over six pounds. The world sauger record of eight pounds, twelve ounces, comes from Lake Sakakawea, North Dakota.[6]

Both walleyes and saugers have slender, tapered heads. The lower jaw is slightly recessed. The sharp teeth that line both jaws are used to grab the fish's prey. However, dental problems among fish, as with their human hunters, vary with the individual. Contrary to popular belief, there is no special time of year when large numbers of walleyes experience aching mouths and widespread loss of teeth. Veteran walleye fishermen, at least the honest ones, have to admit seeing few, if any, toothless walleye specimens. Walleyes do not chew their food, they swallow it whole, and are seldom discouraged from biting because of sore mouths.

Gill covers on walleyes are firm and sharp and can easily inflict cuts on a careless hand. It should be noted that the walleye's gill rakers, those light-colored structures to which the red gill filaments are attached, are not very sharp. Because of this, the angler can reach his finger through the gills to dislodge a hook — as long as he watches out for those gill covers.

The eye has a chocolate-colored iris circled by a narrow

Beautiful walleyes from Lake Sakakawea above the Garrison Dam on the Missouri River in North Dakota. Note the white spot at the tail tip and the black blotch at the base of the front dorsal fin, both distinguishing characteristics of walleyes.

golden margin next to the pupil, and a large, milky blue cornea. The eyes are prominent on the fish's head and have a pearly or glassy appearance. At night, when caught in the glare of a flashlight, a walleye's eyes glow much like those of a cat. When a night fisherman first brings a four-pounder into the beam of his flashlight, those eyes are both eerie and beautiful.

Scientific studies point out that the adult walleye's eye is adapted to dim light conditions and is inadequately equipped to compensate for large differences in light intensity. As a result, larger walleyes often remain in murky, deep, or shaded waters during hours of sunlight. Similar studies have shown that from the time walleyes are hatched until they reach a length of about 1.5 inches, they can be attracted to light at night. Very small walleyes seem to have little aversion to light, since they spend their first couple months on the open lake near the surface, and in shallow water near shore in early summer.[7]

The fact that adult walleyes are shy of light is also borne out by the practical experience of fishermen. They often find walleyes most active in shallow water when the lake is rough, making the water murky, or at night. Combine a cloudy sky with that rough murky water and you regularly experience an upturn in shallow water fishing. Of course, there are times when walleyes do not bite in any water, shallow or deep, regardless of weather conditions.

Sight seems to play an important role in the walleye's quest for food, but how heavily the walleye relies on sight in his feeding is uncertain. If he depends exclusively on sight, the fisherman could expect to catch nothing in turbid, murky waters. He could also anticipate meager results at night. But the fact is that anglers do catch walleyes in cloudy water, and on starless nights as well. This suggests that walleyes depend on their senses of sound, taste, and smell, as well as on sight, for capturing food.

A possible demonstration of the importance of sight in

the walleye's feeding habits is the claim by Mille Lacs Lake harbor fishermen that "the lights have to be on" before significant numbers of the fish enter lagoons at night on autumn feeding sprees. It could be that the light intensity created by the harbor lights is less than that of a very cloudy, even foggy day, when walleyes are most active in shallows. When the harbor lights are on at night there is enough light for sight feeding, but not too much light for the sensitive walleye.

In the fall of 1971, I attempted to test this light theory by fishing six consecutive nights at a harbor on the west shore of Mille Lacs. On two occasions the powerful lights at the harbor entrance were off; on one of them I caught nothing, and on the other I caught two small walleyes. I caught fish on each of the four nights when the lights were on. One evening the lights weren't turned on until more than an hour after dark. Until then I never had a strike. During the next hour, with the lights on, I caught five walleyes. Whether or not my successes and failures in this harbor were related to the lights being on remains an interesting question to ponder. If sight is the key sense used by the walleye to catch his food, then there would have to be enough murkiness in the water to disperse the sun's light during the day and enough water clarity to help the fish find food during the darker hours.

From the diary in which I record my angling experiences, there are several that lend support to the proposition that walleyes are light-shy. These same experiences also seem to indicate that walleyes do not rely entirely on sight to capture food. One such happening was on June 8, 1968, a Saturday. The spring of 1968 was wet and the creeks along the north shore of Mille Lacs poured large quantities of brownish water from the woods and swamps into the lake, causing patches of "brown water" to occur where creeks or ditches enter the lake. That weekend, my dad, brother Steve, and I were guiding a group of St. Paul school teachers on their annual walleye expedition. Mille Lacs walleyes are still inshore at that time and most of our fishing is near the resort.

My strategy that Saturday was based on our accidental success Friday evening after the fellows arrived at the place and got unpacked. We had split up into three small boats. An east wind made it nice for drifting along the shoreline area. Somehow the boat had been allowed to drift into the shallows where there was less than six feet of water. About the time I realized I was in that close, my partners doubled up on walleyes. We stayed in that shallow water and filled out on nice fish. So did the rest of our group in the other boats. More than once we commented on the brown water caused by the discharge of nearby creeks.

By Saturday morning the south wind had started to boil into the fishing grounds, and after some talk about how rough it was, we plowed down to the stretch we had been fishing. The spot was directly out from the harbor mouth at Barneveld's resort. Brant "Barney" Barneveld must have had the same idea, because he started trolling with his launch right outside the harbor. There we were, trolling in water as shallow as three feet, having fish on all the time. The fact that we neglected to put on lighter sinkers for that shallow water made little difference. We caught most of the walleyes right down from the boat. A lift of the pole tip after setting the hook brought walleyes into the landing net — without a crank of the reel! Barney experienced similar luck in those shallows, fishing with a group of a dozen noisy passengers on a party boat nearly forty feet long.

We've rarely enjoyed similar success in that depth of water in daylight hours. Looking back, however, there seems to be a logical explanation for our luck. The water was murky in the shallows because of the wave action, added darkness came from the brown swamp water flowing in from the creeks, and it was cloudy. The amount of light shining through that water was much less than usual. Those walleyes must have had a field day invading the shallows in such comfortably dark water, which they ordinarily find only at night or in deep water.

That good fishing experience and others like it under similar conditions demonstrate that walleyes must find food through the use of more than one sense. If sight alone guides walleyes to food, that dark water would have been disastrous for them. As it was, a week of turbid water yielded some of the season's best fishing.

Another reason why feeding walleyes seem to be only partially dependent on sight is that dark-colored lures are often most effective at night. In his book *Minnesota Fish and Fishing,* Kit Bergh emphasizes the "rule" that light-colored lures have more fish appeal during the day, especially on clear days, and that darker lures are preferred in the evening and at night. In the same chapter, however, Bergh warns fishermen to apply this rule with an open mind and with "an eye for exceptions."[8] The veteran walleye angler views every so-called rule with skepticism.

It seems fair to say that light intensity plays a role in determining *where* walleyes are at a given time. This role may be somewhat diminished when walleyes inhabit relatively deep water, such as bars, reefs, and mud flats where water exceeds twenty feet. A study of fish activity patterns on Lake of the Woods conducted by Kenneth D. Carlander suggests that light intensity affects walleye movement activity on a daily basis.

In Carlander's study, fish were collected in gill nets of various mesh size. These nets were lifted at one, two, and three hour intervals. By converting the catch data to the number of fish caught per hour for a given length of net, Carlander was able to determine the frequency with which each species was caught at different times of the day. It was assumed that the more active a fish became, the more he moved around, the more likely he would be caught in the nets. Nets were set in various depths and areas of the lake, since it was suspected that fish would be in different places at different times. A similar study of fish movement was conducted by Robert E. Cleary on Clear Lake in Iowa. Both studies were later combined and yield interesting information.[9]

In both Lake of the Woods and Clear Lake, walleyes were taken more frequently at night, suggesting that walleyes move around more at this time. Differences in the catch numbers were most evident in shallow water, indicating that walleyes come into the shallows to feed at night. At Clear Lake the greatest activity was at dusk and at dawn, times apparently when walleyes move into and out of their feeding areas in the shallows.

On Lake of the Woods, research showed that light intensity affected daytime walleye activity. On two successive days, when nets were set in shallow water where walleyes were almost never caught during the day, a shower and dark sky occurred at midday. On both of these days, walleyes were caught in the shallow water nets, but only during the hours of rain and overcast. No walleyes were taken there during the other lighter times of these two days. Differences in light intensity closely accompanied this movement pattern.

Granted, it is possible that the storm excited the fish into moving. However, one would expect that the noise and disturbance of a storm, if affecting fish at all, would drive them into deeper water rather than into the shallows. Carlander and Cleary conclude that differences in movement activity of fish on a daily basis is due to light intensity, water temperature (which varies from hour to hour in shallow water), feeding requirements, and certain rhythmic cycles inherent in the fish.[10]

The angler is reminded that the use of the words "active" and "activity" here refer to movement of the fish, not necessarily to feeding activity and the fish's willingness to bite. It is possible that no fish will be caught during the active movement times, while chances are equally good for making impressive catches during the day when walleyes are less likely to be on the move.

Seasonally, the walleye moves or migrates in spring and fall. Spring movements are generally associated with entering and leaving the spawning grounds. Changes in water temperature apparently trigger inshore and offshore movements in autumn. Some observers note that these active movement times coincide with the best fishing.

Most members of the perch family, including the walleye, regularly touch bottom for most of the day. Scuba divers at various lakes have observed walleyes resting motionless on the bottom during daylight hours. They also report that other walleyes may be seen swimming at these times, in deeper water or in cloudier shallow water. The yellow perch, while usually caught close to the bottom, seems to spend more time swimming during the day. But the perch has inactive periods, usually at night, when he rests on the bottom.

For a number of reasons, fishermen expect to find walleye concentrations over clean hard bottom types, such as rocky reefs, hardpan, or clean sand. Walleyes prefer gravel bottoms for spawning. Reefs harbor emerging insects, crustaceans, and small food fish. Researchers believe that the daily resting requirements of walleyes may tend to limit them to such areas. And possibly because of their preference for high oxygen concentrations, walleyes generally avoid silty or muddy bottoms that are often low in oxygen, especially when currents are slight.

There are some mud and silt bottoms, however, that are magnificent walleye havens year after year. Take the mud flats of Mille Lacs, for example. These "flats" are plateaus of very mushy organic material, varying in size and shape, and scattered across the big lake. A few mud flats are within a couple miles of shore. Others are further out in the lake. Water depth on these flats ranges from about twenty to thirty feet, usually averaging about twenty-five feet. The flats are surrounded by hard bottom and deeper water. Each year, during the summer months, nearly all of the walleye fishing on this renowned walleye lake is done on the *mud!*

Perhaps Mille Lacs has currents related to wave action, spring action, and temperature differences, these currents being sufficient to insure an adequate oxygen supply for walleyes throughout most of the lake, regardless of bottom type. A diver who probed the mud of a typical flat and found that it was "like sticking my arm into an iceberg," suggested that cold springs might be present in the mud flat structures. Also suggestive of spring action and oxygen input is the appearance of bubbles rising to the water's surface over the mud flat areas. The bubbles could also be the result of gases created by decomposition of organic materials on the bottom.

In certain walleye lakes, muddy areas harbor aquatic animals of various kinds, along with larvae and nymphs of insects such as the burrowing mayfly. These small organisms sometimes provide food for the walleye and also for small perch, minnows, and tullibees, which in turn attract walleyes.

Thus, even though it is popular to associate walleyes with harder bottom types, one must realize that given proper oxygen and food supplies, walleyes will inhabit mud and silt bottom areas in large numbers for extended periods of time. Remember, too, that walleyes inhabit the water above the bottom, independent of bottom type, and retain their fine eating qualities even over mud.

The walleye has a rather wide temperature tolerance. The northern limits of the walleye range have a mean July temperature of fifty-seven degrees. The water temperature in McIvar Arm of Great Bear Lake never rises much above that level. On the other hand, walleyes are found in rivers, such as the Rock River in Illinois, where they must endure water temperatures as high as the mid-eighties for long periods. Thus, light intensity is even more important than temperature in determining depth chosen by walleyes in summer.[11]

Fishermen often ask which water temperature makes walleyes bite the best. This is hard to answer. In fact, there is probably no specific water temperature that induces walleyes to bite. In Minnesota walleyes are taken through the ice in January, and from considerably warmer waters in mid-July. They can be pulled from deep cold water and from shallow warmer water.

Temperature influences when walleyes enter or leave certain fishing grounds. Aside from drawing walleyes into spawning areas, temperature changes are associated with walleye movement between deep and shallow water on a daily basis, as already pointed out, and, to an unknown extent, on a seasonal basis. It has been mentioned that walleyes move into shallow water at night when the water is frequently several degrees cooler than it is during the day. Temperature has some bearing on the activity of the food fish on which walleyes depend.[12]

Cool autumn weather is apparently needed to draw fish back to the shallows after a warm summer has kept them in deeper regions of the lakes. However, walleye fishermen exaggerate the need for that all-important first frost. Certainly a week of forty-degree weather cools the water more than one night of freezing temperatures. Dock and harbor fishing is best in spring and fall when water is cool. Keep in mind, too, that the autumn and spring periods of cool water temperatures coincide with fewer hours of daylight. So the two important factors of temperature and light intensity interact in their influence on walleye movement.

The fact that temperature is extremely important in determining the commencement of tullibee spawning runs in the bigger northern walleye lakes also has consequences for walleyes. During the tullibee run, very few walleyes are associated with the tullibees. Either walleyes are disturbed by the spawning tullibees or the same water temperature that lures the tullibees into spawning jolts the walleyes out of the same places. Fisheries biologist Fritz Johnson found that at Big Winnie (Lake Winnibigoshish), when fall water temperatures dropped into the 44 to 48 degree range, walleyes suddenly moved offshore.[13]

In the fall of 1970, the annual gill net fishery for tullibees at Mille Lacs was slated to start about October 30. However, the water temperature was still too warm for the tullibee run in some areas of the lake and attention was focused on the good fall walleye fishing that was still going on, to the surprise of many. Because of the large numbers of walleyes in the shallows, the tullibee netting season was postponed until November 6. On November 8 my party fished in the shallow water where limits had been taken the last week in October, and twelve man-hours of angling produced only two walleyes. The tullibee netters were getting tubs full of their fish in these places, but no walleyes. Whatever the reason, years of observation have shown that when the temperature is just right in mid-autumn, the tullibees move in to spawn and the walleyes politely depart.

Walleyes are prolific spawners. Mature females, generally over fifteen inches long, lay from 35 thousand to 600 thousand eggs, depending partially on the female's size. As many as 612 thousand eggs have been found in a single Lake Erie female walleye. The average is around 60 thousand. Often over 90 percent of the eggs are initially fertile. Depending on weather and on bottom structure of the spawning grounds, between 5 and 35 percent of the eggs reach fry stage, less than two inches long. State fisheries crews supplement Minnesota's large natural crop of walleyes with a spawn-taking and hatchery program that produces between four and six million fingerlings annually. Similar, though less extensive, programs exist in other walleye states.

Female walleyes deposit between 35,000 and 600,000 eggs on an annual spring spawning run. Females grow faster, larger, and older than males. Spawn-taking stations are designed to intercept concentrations of spawning walleyes. Many state and provincial conservation departments operate walleye hatchery and stocking programs. Walleyes are easy and inexpensive to reproduce.

In the Minnesota area, the spawning season for walleyes is in late April and early May, usually right after ice-out when the first warm weather raises water temperatures to the low forties. River spawning begins a couple weeks earlier. In Tennessee reservoirs, walleyes spawn from early March into May, being most active the first part of April. There, as in the northern states, spawning commences when water temperatures reach the low forties.[14] In all regions, the timing and length of the spawning run depend on weather conditions. Males are first to reach the spawning areas and are last to leave, this being the reason for a disproportionate number of the smaller males in early spring catches.

Lake walleyes are famous as "stream spawners" because these stream spawning runs are conspicuous. However, most walleye spawning takes place in the lakes along shallow shoreline areas and on shallow reefs and shoals where wave action keeps the water in motion. Prospective spawners lie in deeper water off the spawning areas during the daytime and move in for spawning at night. Spawning occurs in water less than four feet deep and as shallow as several inches. Shoals of gravel and small rock are most preferred and yield the best hatches. Walleyes also spawn on sand and, to a much lesser extent, over mud and submerged weeds. Unlike many panfish and bass, the walleye is not a nest builder.

In walleye spawning runs, the smaller males outnumber the females by three and four to one. A female is accompanied by one or more of the males. Male and female pull alongside each other. With a slight tilt of their bodies, anal vents are brought close together and eggs from females and milt from males are emitted. When a number of fish are present there is quite a commotion in the water.

The walleye eggs are left unattended and are randomly scattered along the bottom. The period of incubation varies with water temperature. The eggs hatch in 26 days when water temperature is 40°F.; 21 days when 50°-55°F.; and

Gravel-rubble shoreline is ideal for walleye spawning. The fish spawn in water as shallow as a few inches and seldom deeper than four feet.

7 days at a mean temperature of 57°F. It is believed that a shorter incubation period produces a better hatch.[15]

Biologists have found that cold weather has a detrimental effect on walleye spawning runs. A sudden drop in water temperature during the spawning run can turn it off almost entirely. A dramatic demonstration of this was found at Heming Lake, Manitoba, about twenty miles south of Sherridon. The lake is three miles long by about a half-mile wide. There, ice-out and spawning are nearly a month behind Minnesota's schedule of such events.

In the spring of 1947 ice left Heming Lake on May 22. Researchers set hoop nets in Heming and Northwest creeks on May 10, intending to monitor the 1947 run of walleye spawners. The first fish moved in on May 14 and 15. Some of the fish, especially the females, were not ready for spawning. At this time males were outnumbering females by four to one, a ratio that remained constant throughout the spawning period. The first eggs were deposited in Northwest Creek on May 20, indicating that the spawning run was definitely in progress. The water temperature was 43 degrees. On May 25 cold weather set in, and it remained cold until June 1. By May 28, after several days of the cold weather, the water temperature dropped to 41 degrees. At the start of the cold snap the spawning walleyes suddenly moved out of the creeks and back into Heming Lake. They had not returned by June 5, even though spawning remained uncompleted.

Later in June, angling in deep water produced female walleyes that were reabsorbing their eggs. It was found that the cold weather resulted in a bad hatch overall, as test seining in July and August revealed absolutely no young-of-the-year walleyes where they were regularly taken in previous years.

The Heming Lake study seems to indicate that walleyes require certain optimum temperature conditions to successfully complete spawning. In this case, after the spawning run had started, a cold spell and the accompanying drop in water temperature drove the walleyes from their spawning activity and completely disrupted that year's reproduction.[16]

A similar study of spawning walleyes was conducted at Knutson Creek in Sawyer County near Birchwood, Wisconsin. Knutson Creek flows into Chetac Lake. Walleyes use a mile and a half of the stream for spawning. Knutson Creek is ten to twenty feet wide and has a depth varying from six inches to two and a half feet. During the study conducted in the spring of 1941, the walleyes entered Knutson Creek in large numbers on the night of April 18. On the following night a severe wind and storm caused the water temperature to drop five and six degrees. The spawning run stopped entirely.

On the night of April 20 a survey of the stream's lower mile and a half was made and no walleyes could be seen. The storm and cold weather had stopped the run. On April 25, with warmer water, another check was made and the stream was found to be loaded with spawning walleyes.[17]

These studies, demonstrating the dramatic effects of cold and stormy weather on walleye spawning runs, are of special interest to anglers. Perhaps there is a relationship between a successfully completed spawning session and good spring walleye fishing. Does bad weather during the spawning time and a broken-up, physiologically upset walleye population result in poor spring fishing? To see if such a relationship exists, it might be worthwhile to compare weather conditions of the spawning period, around May 1, with fishing results of the first several weeks of the walleye season in May and early June. To be at all conclusive, such an investigation would have to cover at least ten years.

Unfortunately, my Mille Lacs fishing diary is too incomplete for a reliable study, especially since it does not contain specific information on when the spawning runs commenced in given years. However, the spring fishing seasons of 1957 and 1964 were generally poor, and not just for a day or so here and there, while 1958 and 1971 brought exceptionally good spring fishing. What kind of weather prevailed during the spawning runs of those years? Would bad weather show up during the spawning runs of 1957 and 1964, years when spring fishing was poor?

I was able to obtain weather information and more fishing notes from neighbors Irene Pieper and her fisherman husband Bob. Irene began her diary when the Piepers moved to the north shore of Mille Lacs in 1956. High and low temperatures and jottings on daily happenings comprise most of the diary. Our findings were interesting. In 1957, ice left the lake on April 27. From then through May 1, the period when spawning was most probably getting under way, the weather was mild. Then cold and windy weather set in for the next several days, frost being observed on the morning of May 4. These cold temperatures, combined with wave action in the shallows where walleyes spawn, undoubtedly lowered the water temperature there and possibly broke up the spawning activity. Fishing was not good that spring.

Similarly, the first week in May of 1964 was cold and windy, and our inshore spring walleye fishing was poor. We did catch a few big walleyes, probably females, in deep water where we seldom fish in spring. It is possible that these fish had their spawning run disrupted by the wind and a drop in water temperature and consequently left the areas where they usually are during the several weeks after spawning. Also, if these fish did not spawn at all, they may have experienced various physiological reactions that discouraged them from biting.

Excellent spring fishing on the north shore of Mille Lacs took place in 1958 and in 1971. In both years there was no sudden drop in water temperature during the spawning time, meaning that walleyes probably completed their spawning. Naturally, more evidence and more thorough investigation on the relationship between normal spawning runs and good spring fishing is needed. In the author's opinion, however, if water temperature influences Opening Day walleye fishing, it is the temperature of the spawning period rather than the temperature reading on the opener that is important.

The completion of a spawning run and the deposition of thousands of eggs cannot in itself insure a bumper crop of young walleyes. There is constant danger throughout the period of incubation prior to hatching and until walleyes grow beyond the fingerling stage. Weather conditions are most critical during the early days. As noted before, fluctuating temperatures can disrupt spawning so that the fish might spawn intermittently over a long period of time. During a cold spring, following an initial warm spell, many walleyes fail to spawn and many eggs spawned late in the season are sterile, simply because they are too old. Heavy winds right after spawning can wash eggs from the ideal bottom and depth into less suitable areas. On the larger lakes, windrows of walleye eggs have been seen along the shorelines following severe windstorms.[18]

It has been mentioned that walleyes are drawn to bottom areas of gravel and small rock for spawning. The importance of bottom type in walleye spawning has been convincingly underscored by Minnesota Department of Natural Resources biologist Fritz Johnson in his study of walleye egg survival on several bottom types at Lake Winnibigoshish.[19] Survival of naturally spawned walleye eggs was determined on five bottom areas of Lake Winnie over a period of four years. The bottom types included muck, sand, gravel, rubble (rocks of three to six inches), and boulders. Each study area was between one thousand and fifteen hundred square feet.

In 1956 Johnson found that egg survival was best on gravel and rubble bottoms, around 25 percent, and as low as 6 percent on muck bottoms. In order to test this observation, 25 cubic yards of pit-run gravel, with rocks of one to six inches in diameter, were spread six inches deep over sand bottom. In 1958 and in 1959 it was found that the abundance of eggs on the "improved" bottom was up to ten times greater than it was before the deposits of gravel were spread over the sand.

Johnson's experiment reinforced the belief that walleyes prefer gravel and rubble for spawning, and that egg survival is greater on these bottoms. The experiment also convinced walleye management teams that improvement of natural spawning areas by deposition of gravel and small rock can in some circumstances be more effective than artificial stocking in maintaining and increasing walleye populations. In lakes where good spawning grounds are lacking, this type of habitat improvement can substantially increase walleye production.

During the first months of a walleye's life, survival depends on ample food and freedom from predator fish. Walleye fry are only one-half inch long at hatching. Soon after hatching, and after the yolk sacs have been absorbed, the tiny fry rise to the lake's surface where they scatter out for several weeks, feeding upon plankton.[20] The fact that these small walleyes are scattered randomly across the lake's surface is to their advantage, since would-be predators are usually deeper, and would probably be attracted only to concentrated populations of the walleye fry. It has been suspected that surface-feeding tullibees might rely on the tiny walleyes for food. However, a study of thirty-five surfacing tullibees (taken in early June, 1960 from Lake Vermilion in northern St. Louis County, Minnesota) found that all were feeding on insects and microcrustaceans. No traces of fish could be found in these stomachs.[21] If walleye fry are plentiful enough in certain waters, they may be open to predation by tullibees.

When walleyes reach a length of 1.2 inches, usually in late June, they begin to feed on small fish, especially young perch of the same year-class. Analysis of first-year walleye populations in a number of lakes has shown that from July to September the young walleyes feed almost entirely on fish. Also at this time, the small walleyes return to the shoreline areas where they spend much of their first summer.

In most walleye lakes, the growth of young walleyes during the first summer is sufficiently more rapid than the growth of perch, so walleyes are able to feed on perch most of the summer. In fact, walleyes are sometimes large enough in August, just several months after hatching, to feed on small year-old perch. If for some reason a large walleye hatch is followed by a limited perch hatch, or if perch grow rapidly to sizes too large for the small walleyes to consume, the year's walleye crop could be greatly reduced. The relationship between walleyes and perch, especially during the first year, cannot be emphasized enough. Data has been collected showing that first-year walleyes grow slower where the year's perch hatch was weak, and that good perch years are usually good walleye years in the typical walleye lake. There is no evidence that young perch compete with young walleyes for food. During the first summer perch feed mainly on crustaceans and insects, while walleyes feed on the perch.

Aside from offering abundant food for baby walleyes, large numbers of small perch start filling the gullets of adult walleyes in early July. Where these perch are numerous they may be the primary cause of slow fishing in middle and late summer. For years walleye fishermen have griped about summer "dog days." Indeed, many walleye anglers simply stay home from mid-June to late September. Traditionally the view has been that warmer waters during the summer months send walleyes into deeper water, where they become harder to find and where they take on the summertime "blahs," hardly moving a fin and being too lazy to eat.

While it is generally true that adult walleyes head for deeper water by the end of June, for whatever reasons, they do not stop feeding. Actually, during that August slump walleyes are feeding more and growing faster than they do at any other time of the year. They are feeding almost exclusively on the year's new perch crop, which averages one inch long by July 1, and 2.2 inches long by August 10.[22] At this time walleyes are feeding on perch to the exclusion of nearly everything else.

Young-of-the-year and yearling perch constitute the bulk of the fish diet of walleyes. Studies demonstrate that in certain lakes (Leech, Mille Lacs, and Winnibigoshish in Minnesota; Gogebic in Michigan; Oneida in New York), yellow perch occur more frequently than any other forage fish in the stomachs of walleyes.

However, walleyes feed most readily on food supplies available to them. In some waters that means reliance on food fish other than yellow perch. Local anglers at Big Stone Lake on the Minnesota-South Dakota border point to large numbers of young silver bass found in walleyes. In Wisconsin, Lake Winnebago walleyes seem to feed on troutperch and freshwater drum more than on yellow perch. In other areas, such as the reservoirs of Tennessee, the gizzard shad is listed as the principal food. Occasionally walleyes consume tullibees, bluegills, bullheads, suckers, burbot, and the young of other fish. Most studies reveal a dependence on the young of larger fish rather than on minnows, although shiners, darters, fatheads, and other minnows are present in the walleye's natural diet. Blood worms and leeches also show up in walleyes.

In most walleye lakes, spring finds walleyes feeding mainly on insects, especially nymphs of burrowing mayflies, and sometimes on minnows such as the common lake or spottail shiner which appears in the shallows in spring to spawn. In late May and early June newly-hatched perch are often less than one-half inch long, and year-old perch are frequently over three inches long. Possibly perch are either too small or too large to be preferred by walleyes in many places early in the fishing season. It is during this time, before the new perch grow large enough to catch the walleye's fancy, that the angler often has his best walleye fishing.

The advance of autumn often brings a reduction in the numbers of "bite size" perch, so the angler stands a better chance of tempting a walleye into striking. This is characteristic of a "normal" walleye fishing year — good in spring and early summer, generally poor in the middle and end of summer, better again in the fall.

Biologist Dennis Schupp discovered that the abundance of young-of-the-year perch in Leech Lake falls off sharply by late September and early October, and he explains that this happens in most walleye lakes in most years.[23] By fall, natural mortality, including consumption of huge numbers of the perch by walleyes, cuts the supply of little perch by 50 percent and more. In some years the population of young perch is well above normal. The supply might be so huge that the summer fishing slump stretches right through the fall months. 1971 was such a year at Lake Mille Lacs. Fishing remained generally poor on the lake all fall. From the shore at Wigwam Bay, Isle, and Wealthwood, and fishing in various harbors on the north and west shores of that lake, endless schools of two- and three-inch perch could be seen in mid-October. In the fall of 1970, by comparison, there appeared to be fewer young perch, and fall fishing was terrific.

In years past, fishermen were mystified when prolonged periods of slow fishing set in. They took for granted that if they failed to catch fish, the fish just weren't around. A lake was said to be "fished out" when that really was not the case at all. Now that more information is available on walleyes, one can begin to see how walleyes are affected by the environment and how this, in turn, affects walleye fishing. Along with daily and hourly changes in barometer, wind, temperature, sky cover — and the fish's moods — more general conditions, such as the quality of a spawning run and the abundance of food fish, can influence walleye fishing in significant ways.

State conservation officials man state-financed hatchery and rearing pond programs that supplement natural walleye hatches. Minnesota leads the nation in artificial walleye production, rearing between four and six million fingerlings annually, along with many millions of fry. Walleyes are easy and inexpensive to produce. While natural hatches often fall below a 10 percent survival rate, state hatchery programs achieve successful hatches of 75 percent and more.

Spawn-taking stations are strategically located at the walleye spawning grounds, usually on streams or narrows between lakes where the spawners can be easily trapped for stripping purposes. Stations at Pine River, Cutfoot Sioux, and the Tamarac River at Waskish are among those that consistently yield huge numbers of walleye eggs in Minnesota. Fisheries workers appear at these stations early in April to prepare for the big runs, which usually occur after ice-out, toward the end of April and early May.

With gentle pressure on the female's belly, eggs are extruded into a pan containing a little water. Milt is added by "forcing" a male in the same way. Fish are never stripped completely. They are returned to their natural environments for completion of spawning. Later a fair share of fry and fingerlings are returned from the hatcheries and ponds to the home waters of the parent fish. Because artificial hatching has a high success ratio, lakes where spawn-taking occurs gain from such practices, in spite of popular misconceptions to the contrary.

It is important to ensure that eggs are fertilized within several minutes after being taken. Eggs and milt are carefully stirred by tilting the pan. This accomplishes fertilization. Then eggs are gently placed in pails of water that contain suspended clay particles. The clay particles adhere to the eggs, which are adhesive the first hour, thus preventing them from massing together.

Females and males are stripped of a portion of their eggs and milt, then released to complete spawning in their native waters. Many lakes and streams which host spawn-taking operations receive fry and fingerlings to compensate for any "loss" due to spawn-taking.

After hardening for an hour or more, the eggs can be transported. At the fisheries headquarters they are placed in battery jars where they will remain separated. To insure their separation and freedom, and to provide aeration, the eggs are kept in motion by a continuous flow of water.

In Minnesota's walleye rearing program, fry from eggs incubated in a hatchery are placed in rearing ponds in May. In these ponds, usually less than fifteen acres in size, the walleyes grow to the fingerling size of two to six inches. After several months in the ponds, the small walleyes are removed for stocking in the lakes.

There are some differences between fingerling walleyes reared in ponds and their young counterparts that are native to the lakes. First of all, in typical walleye lakes there is a near balance of males and females, with females slightly outnumbering males in some instances. In the ponds, however, males outnumber females at an average of six to four, some ponds yielding up to 90 percent males. The reasons for this are largely unknown. It seems probable that certain environmental factors in rearing ponds, including fish population density, cause this preponderance of males.[24] Since mature females grow faster and eventually get larger than males, it is desirable that as many stocked walleyes as possible be females. Perhaps when biologists learn why males are more numerous in rearing ponds, they will be able to influence the sex ratio of pond-reared walleyes in a way that will benefit the fish and the fisherman.

Secondly, walleyes from ponds are smaller than those that spend infancy in the lakes. In some cases there is the question of how successfully these smaller fish can compete with lake-produced walleyes. It is possible that adding walleyes from rearing ponds to natural walleye lakes can be a wasteful practice, since the smaller pond fish are at a disadvantage in competition for food.[25]

Walleyes are considered a fast-growing fish, for good reason. Studies indicate that a three-pound walleye eats in

After fertilization and hardening, eggs are placed in battery jars and are kept in motion by a continuous flow of water.

the neighborhood of three thousand small fish each year. He digests his food rapidly. While he eats more and grows faster in summer, he feeds during the winter and can be caught in rewarding numbers through the ice. Females grow faster and get larger than males. And since most big wall-eyes are females, it is supposed that females live longer too. Males mature earlier, when they are 12-13.5 inches long and 2-3 years old. Females mature at 15-17 inches and 4-5 years old, earlier in southern regions.

By the end of their first August, fingerling walleyes are about five inches long, and are over six inches long by the following May. Fishermen often question the age and weight of the walleyes they catch. As a rule, a twelve-inch walleye weighs about a half a pound and is between two and three years old; an eighteen-inch walleye is just short of two pounds and is five years old; a twenty-one incher is about three pounds and seven years old. A five-pounder is about twenty-five inches long, and for each inch after that you can add a pound. Thus, your ten-pound walleye will measure about thirty inches long, and he will be at least eleven or twelve years old.

This length-weight relationship is pretty reliable. But in some waters it takes longer for walleyes to reach a certain size. Growth rates are determined by abundance of food fish, water temperature, and fish population size. Fishing pressure by sportsmen and commercial harvesters also in-fluences the average size of the fish. In many Minnesota walleye waters, a pound-and-a-half walleye is between four and five years old. In Red Lake, a walleye the same size is seven or eight years old, showing a significantly slower growth rate for that lake.[26]

Among adult walleye populations that receive a fair amount of fishing pressure there is a natural death toll of about 5 percent. Natural mortality rises to as high as 30 percent where fishing pressure is minimal.[27] These figures seem to tell us that in the absence of fishing pressure, just

A pair of 5-pound walleyes measuring close to 25 inches. Generally, a pound can be added for each inch of nicely proportioned walleye larger than 25 inches and 5 pounds. A 28-inch walleye weighs about 8 pounds, for example. "Skinny" and "fat" walleyes may upset this inch-pound relationship.

about as many walleyes would die anyway. According to the Minnesota Department of Natural Resources, between 20 and 30 percent of keeper-size walleyes are caught in most years on the popular walleye lakes.[28] On these lakes, where there is a steady fishing pressure from year to year, the major cause of adult walleye mortality is angling.

Apparently walleyes are quite immune to epidemics of fatal diseases. Studies reveal no accounts of mass deaths among groups of walleyes due to disease or parasite infestations. Leeches will occasionally attach themselves to a walleye's head, but these are harmless. Walleyes seldom carry the yellowish-white grubs that sometimes infest perch. When these worms are found in walleyes their numbers are small. While unsightly, these worms are harmless to man.

"Fish lice," particularly little flat specimens about a quarter-inch across, are occasionally seen on walleyes. They concentrate on the back of the fish directly behind the head. These little creatures are known to create raw spots on the walleyes where they concentrate long enough, possibly weakening the fish. It seems that in seasons where the lice are present, their numbers diminish after a few weeks and they claim few if any victims from the schools of walleyes.[29]

Warts and unsightly pinkish growths cause walleye anglers to wonder if the fish is sick or if they too will get warts from handling the affected fish. Skin warts of varying sizes may occur almost anywhere on the fish's body, but most often on gill covers and fins. The most common wart, seen especially in spring, is due to the lymphocystis virus. This virus is widespread among fish throughout the world, in both salt and fresh water. It has been reported from many species of a wide range of fish families, including various food fish and even tropical aquarium fish. There are few species in which lymphocystis is common. In the United States this disease has been reported consistently only among walleyes. Occurrence ranges from a small fraction of 1 percent to 5 percent or more. The first reports of lymphocystis, in a walleye from Wisconsin, were not published until 1918. Yet some old fishermen tell of warts on walleyes as far back as they can remember.

At first, the warts are firm and lumpy. Later the surface breaks and the wart becomes more loosely textured, eventually sloughing off. The skin scars over. The virus is contagious among the walleyes and is "free" in the water. It attacks individual fish when the skin surface has been broken. That is why warts are most common on the exposed parts of the fish, such as fins, gill covers, and lips. One fish can have from one to dozens of the warts. Even the large warts are almost never more than skin deep.

Some walleyes obtained for study have carried warts diagnosed as skin sarcomas, a type of tumor with a cellular structure different from that of the lymphocystis warts. Regardless of what kind of wart his walleye has, the fisherman can relax. The warts are harmless to man. Warty walleyes can be filleted and eaten just like the others.[30]

Since walleyes inhabit open waters and relatively deep waters throughout their lives, they seldom are the prey of bird and mammal predators. They are too big for most birds, although cases of adult walleyes being taken by eagles and herons have been reported.[31]

Evidence of how old walleyes can get is found in the exceptional case of a female walleye at Bemidji. This fish was first taken during the spawning run of 1918. It then weighed twelve pounds. It reappeared in nearly every consecutive spawning run through 1929. It weighed 17.5 pounds and was between eighteen and twenty years old when last reported. Minnesota's record walleye is 16.5 pounds. The world's record, from Tennessee, is 25 pounds and approximately three feet long. Weights over ten pounds are rare, and walleyes over five pounds are considered "big."[32]

Professional guide and tackle manufacturer Al Lindner and a proud guest display "hog" walleyes.

PART 2
WALLEYE FISHING

Throughout their range, walleyes are treasured by anglers. Reasons for this are as varied as they are personal. The walleye is a clean-looking delicious specimen that fillets out easily. This fish can be caught in both lakes and streams by many diverse methods. Jigging with spinning gear, still-fishing with a cane pole and bobber, deepwater trolling with heavy tackle, ice fishing — you name it. Anglers with completely different fishing styles can share the pleasures of catching walleyes in a variety of settings.

The walleye is a wanderer. He inhabits different areas of lakes and streams as days and seasons progress. Walleyes are moody biters. They are particular and touchy, so the angler must be creative and meticulous in presenting his baits. Overall, walleyes have an unpredictable nature which makes them interesting and challenging to pursue. A walleye fisherman conditions himself to his quarry's deceptive ways and is ready to endure a succession of failures. At the same time, his triumphs are sweet. A limit catch of nice walleyes stirs special pride in any angler and unlimited envy among his friends. Once conditioned, the walleye angler is hooked for life.

Northern and bass partisans regard the walleye as a

sluggish and tired fighter. While it is true that they seldom break water and cut capers like more renowned battlers, walleyes have probably been underrated in this regard. Walleyes are powerful swimmers and are capable of overtaking a largemouth bass. They have no trouble catching their prey and will strike fast-moving lures. Walleyes caught on light tackle provide great sport. And bringing a fish up from the depths, where walleyes often are, is a thrill any time.

For decades, walleye fishing has been characterized by traditional approaches and old "rules," characteristically static and clear-cut. By offering no alternatives, they limited the angler's growth as a true and accomplished fisherman. Now, successful walleye fishermen are finally admitting that flexibility is often the key to success — that there is more to walleye fishing than narrow stereotypes about the fish, one lure, one wind, and one lake. Discovering that nearly every rule has its exceptions, that an approach used successfully one day may be lousy the next, that the "best" lake may be the worst one at times, and that walleyes aren't always sluggish, bottom-pushing night feeders, usually means a new life for the fisherman.

A versatile angler, one who can change from spinning tackle to heavy trolling gear or from plugs to night crawlers, as conditions might require, is a more consistent producer of walleye strings than his one-way, one-minded neighbor. Being able to adapt to a variety of fishing environments, conditions, and tackle is the mark of maturity for the walleye enthusiast.

Walleye fishing has changed over the last twenty years. The emphasis on monofilament line has had wide implications. The advent and growth of jigging in the fifties and early sixties, along with the increased popularity of spinning gear, has made walleye fishing tackle considerably lighter than it used to be. Wire leaders and big swivel-snaps, spinners on lengths of heavy wire, big hooks, and clumsy plugs have all but disappeared. Lightweight Finnish plugs have come on the scene hard and fast. Lindy Rigs employ small hooks that defy the old-timers who can hardly see them. Little Joe Red Devil spinners with blades mounted directly on monofilament leaders have revolutionized spinner fishing. Even many party boat fishermen have lengthened their leaders and filled their big reels with clear monofilament line.

The ice fisherman uses lighter line, smaller hooks, smaller sinkers, and smaller bobbers. The river fisherman is now seen with spinning gear and more refined terminal tackle. The shore fisherman with his bottom line demonstrates the advantages of a sliding sinker which "the fish can't even feel."

Astounding numbers of boats and snowmobiles give the fisherman a new mobility on our lakes and streams, summer and winter. Fishing has been made more comfortable by these plush transportation vehicles and by welcomed advances in the outdoor clothing industry. Ice augers powered by batteries and gas engines make chopping a hole sound tougher than it really is. Electronic equipment gives fishermen depth and temperature readings with the flick of a switch. Nowadays the sport seems to involve much more than just "going fishing."

The modern walleye fisherman must learn how to sift through these new rigs and lures lining the walls of bait shops — and the rules, both old and new — for the most effective means of catching walleyes. At first the novice walleye angler might be scared away from the sport by the vast array of lures, baits, methods, and theories that make up walleye fishing. With that in mind, the purpose of the following pages is to discuss and illustrate, in a comprehensive and orderly way, the techniques and theories of modern walleye fishing.

Some Common Walleye Fishing Rigs

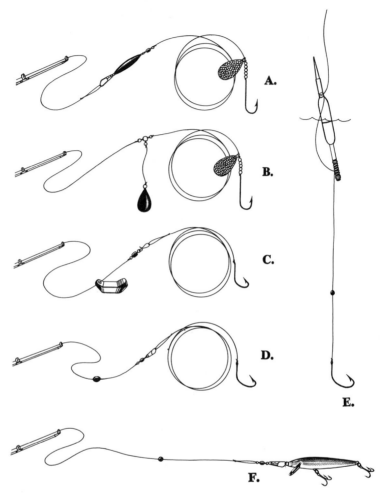

A. A "straight" hook-up for trolling and drifting, featuring swivel sinker and spinner, used with minnows, night crawlers, and other live bait. **B.** A 3-way rig for deep trolling. Leader material for spinner or other baits should be in the 10 to 15 pound test range (monofilament), somewhat lighter for drop to sinker. **C.** The Lindy Rig, with "walking" sinker and plain hook, used for drifting and slow trolling minnows, crawlers, leeches, and other live bait. **D.** A popular sliding egg sinker-plain hook outfit for bottom fishing from shore or dock. **E.** A typical still-fishing approach with bobber, split shot, and plain hook. Especially effective when ice fishing. Minnows hooked just under dorsal fin. **F.** The Rapala rigged for evening or night trolling, using split-shot weight about 15 inches ahead of lure. Use 6 to 12 pound test monofilament throughout, with no wire leaders.

OLD NOTIONS IN REVIEW

For many years, probably as far back as the earliest walleye fishing goes, a collection of old sayings has governed the approaches and attitudes of countless walleye fishermen. Anglers have taken for granted that "the rougher it is the better," that "when the wind is from the west the fish bite the best," that thunderstorms drive walleyes into seemingly bottomless depths where they remain frightened and inactive for a day or even a week.

Fishermen take these theories seriously enough so that their confidence in a fishing situation depends on them. They may even stay home simply because the lake is too calm or because it thundered the night before. The problem with these standard notions about walleye fishing is that most of them are unreliable.

Remember, the walleye is a creature of the primitive outdoor world, governed by his hunger and sex drives and by fear. For him, the name of the game is survival. The walleye plays his survival game amidst uncertainties of all kinds — changing temperatures and light conditions, rising and falling water levels, abundance of food, fluctuating oxygen supplies, quality of the water, barometric pressures, wind, waves, and currents. Study and experience can explain how walleyes tend to react when faced with certain conditions of nature, and sometimes one can see what seem to be discernible patterns of behavior, however crooked those patterns might be. But beware of the fisherman who claims to know everything about walleyes. Nobody has all the answers.

Let us examine some of the traditional thinking about walleyes and walleye fishing, keeping in mind that the old "rules" are often misleading and must be broken in order to catch fish consistently.

The rougher it is the better. Nonsense! Go walleye fishing anytime, as long as it isn't too rough. Hundreds of thousands of walleyes are caught each year, during the day and night, in cloudiness and in sunshine, in deep and shallow water, when the water is glassy calm. However, there are some patterns here.

It is true that waves sometimes make a difference for the better, particularly in shallow water less than twelve feet deep. In shallow water, heavy wave action oxygenates the water right down to the bottom where the fish are. Waves put life into the water and into the fish. The turbulent water brings small organisms and particles into suspension, causing minnows and other food fish to be more active in the shallows, which in turn attracts more walleyes. Waves rile the water, making it murky and more tolerable for the light-sensitive walleye. It is very often true that wave action brings greater concentrations of walleyes into water less than ten feet deep, provided the fish are within reasonable distance of these shallow areas in the first place. However, the fact that fish are present is no guarantee that you'll catch them. They simply may not bite for any number of reasons, regardless of your approach, and waves are no assurance that walleyes will bite either, even in the shallows.

A series of privately published lake contour maps features "fishing tips" on the reverse sides. One "tip" is that walleyes head for the rough side of the lake when it's windy. Incredible! Walleyes from Big Winnie's north shore heading across the lake whenever the north wind blows? A mass migration from Garrison to Isle at Mille Lacs? No, of course not. But the fish that are already at the rough ends of those big lakes might bite better, making it seem like that's where all the fish are. While this well-intentioned tip might hold some truth on small lakes, given the same wind for days on end, it obviously bears no relevance to bigger lakes, especially when walleyes are deep. Summer walleyes don't suddenly leave their deep water bars and flats and scurry miles toward shore to romp in the waves when a wind comes up. And being as deep as they are on those big lakes, there seems to be no reason why waves twenty or thirty feet above them should influence their willingness to bite.

Hardy fishermen like to fish in the waves and catch more fish when it's rough because they wisely put the waves to work for them. Waves, or rather the wind, can be a great help to drift fishermen, since wind accounts for as much boat movement as the waves do. The right wind can keep the boat where it ought to be over a bar, flat, or shoreline area. In spring and fall, for example, when the walleyes are close to shore in some of my favorite lakes, I enjoy fishing in heavy wind over shallow water. There is a certain ruggedness about it that appeals to me and walleyes often bite in that choppiness. But years of experience in many walleye lakes have proved to me that rough water is no guarantee that the fish will bite.

Furthermore, when general conditions such as an abundant natural food supply turn fishing off for weeks or even months, the wind, regardless of direction, velocity, or wave size, will do little to influence fishing results.

Then why "the rougher the better"? Well, the hardnosed proponents of that theory are usually of the older school of walleye fishermen. Years ago, walleye angling was generally limited to shoreline areas, especially on the bigger lakes. Back then a lack of knowledge about the lakes and the lack of reliable boats and motors prevented fishermen from exploiting bars and flats far from shore. Fishing was often confined to the shallows in spring and in fall. Because they fished in the shallows, fishermen had better luck when the lake was rough. The same thing happens today.

At Mille Lacs, for example, those who remember say that, prior to the late 1930s, many resorts pulled their fleets of rowboats out of the water in late June because there were "no fish." Then in September they'd go back to fishing. The reason why there were "no fish" is that the fish moved out to the mud flats in late June and stayed there until fall. In more recent years Mille Lacs walleye fishing keeps going through the summer because fishermen move out to the mud flats along with the walleyes. Fishermen who regularly fish the flats find that hot calm days sometimes produce the best catches, but years ago, fishermen didn't know about that.[1]

When the wind is from the west they bite the best. Guides hear this line from their customers almost every day. When the wind's from the east they're supposed to bite the least; when it's from the north few fishermen sally forth; and when the wind is from the south it's supposed to blow the hook right into the fish's mouth!

There is rhyme to this, but very little reason. A west wind might be ideal for drifting the length of your favorite shore-line or drop-off area. Fine. But maybe a north wind can accomplish the same thing when you're fishing somewhere else. There is no real pattern; that "good wind" for you on one side of a lake might be disastrous for me on the opposite side. The ideal wind can be a north wind in one situation, a south wind in another. Sometimes you see consistency in a certain wind when fishing a spot. Keep that in mind for future reference. But don't be surprised if it fails to work all the time. And by all means keep quiet when they're talking wind at a lake you hit for the first time, because your wind might be the wrong one there, even if it blows from the west.

For example, I have caught limits of walleyes in east winds as often as I've lucked out in westerlies. In fact, west winds are often associated with the passage of a cold front that can cause temporary lulls in the action, even during the best weeks of the walleye season. During the first few days of June, 1971, I had some of my best walleye fishing ever, in a heavy east wind!

I go by the barometer. If your barometer out-guesses wall-eyes consistently, it's worth a good price! Not that walleyes aren't influenced by changes in barometric pressure; they are. How they react is the question. This is the point where our theories, fellow anglers, get shot down in a hurry.

Traditionally, it has been assumed that a falling barometer means slower fishing and that a rising barometer means more fish. A few believe strongly in the opposite. Storms, most of them say, spell bad fishing for their duration and for some time after. Thunder and violent weather, they claim, drive walleyes into deep water where they remain for some time, scared and with little appetite. People and animals are frightened by storms. Fish are known to spook for a variety of reasons, so why shouldn't they be really jolted by a rousing thunderstorm?

Maybe they are. Maybe walleyes react to thunder by not feeding — *sometimes*. There may also be times when it prods them into being more active. Most full-time walleye anglers admit that there is no really consistent pattern of bad fishing during and after thunderstorms. Both limit catches and "skunkings" occur before, during, and after thunderstorms, and with rising, falling, and steady barometer readings.

One of my most memorable days of walleye fishing was at my father's resort on Mille Lacs, June 24, 1966. We had experienced a week of stable weather and moderately good fishing. We felt that continued good luck might be upset by heavy winds and stormy weather, especially at this critical time in late June when the Mille Lacs walleyes leave the shoreline areas and head for the mud flats further out in the lake. At about eleven on the night of the twenty-third, we went into seven hours of gusty wind, nearly three inches of rain, and intense thunder and lightning activity. As we left the harbor on our 8:00 A.M. fishing trip on the following day, it was still cloudy, with the dull rumble of thunder in the distance.

That morning we fished about half a mile west of the resort, in ten to fifteen feet of water not far from shore. To our amazement, the walleyes went wild. We limited out for our party of seven — forty-two beautiful walleyes — despite the thunder, and despite the earlier grumbling of several fishermen who expected the fishing to be "dead" after that storm.

Later that day we gambled and took nine Mankato anglers out to a flat about three miles offshore, going right past where we got the fish in the morning. The result was over seventy walleyes in two and a half hours, including a limit of fifty-four good keepers for the gang.

We've had better days, but that one followed a real ripper of a thunderstorm. And it was dead calm. Once more the old-timers' slogans were dashed by biting walleyes.

Walleyes are night feeders. For some reason, most published descriptions of the walleye lead one to believe that he should fish for walleyes only at night. The walleye is characterized as a night feeder. Yet probably more than 90 percent of the walleyes caught in Leech, Winnie, Mille Lacs, and other walleye lakes are caught during the day. Most guides work only during daylight hours. Walleyes do bite at night, and this makes the sport of catching them all the more interesting, but night fishing is seldom better than daytime fishing in the long run.

In autumn, dock fishing and harbor fishing can pay off when a day in the boat produces nothing. Trolling after dark, especially on the smaller walleye lakes, sometimes breaks the summer slump. Night-feeding walleyes concentrate on sand and gravel bars in the rivers, particularly where feeder streams join the main flow, and sometimes bite pretty well.

Most night fishing for walleyes is confined to less than ten feet of water, since walleyes move into the shallows at night unless they're concentrated on bars or flats some distance out on the lake, where they often are in summer. Remember that only at certain times and in select places

Dock fishermen often assemble an hour or two before dark and fish until midnight. Favorite tackle includes plain hook rigs with sliding sinkers for minnows and frogs, as well as jig-minnow combinations.

does the darkness of night mean more walleyes on the stringer.

Drag bottom for walleyes. Adult walleyes are nearly always found within three feet of the bottom. Migrating walleyes have been spotted by ice fishermen swimming as high as ten feet above the bottom and only six feet below the ice, but these present a special case, a real exception, because few walleyes are taken at or near the surface. On walleye lakes in northern Minnesota, schools of surface-feeding tullibees break water on calm summer days and are mistaken for walleyes. Anglers do catch walleyes in shallow water, using no sinkers. But whether this is done with live bait or with diving plugs, the fish are caught near the bottom. One of the few rules that holds true for walleye fishermen almost all of the time is that he must fish *near* the bottom, though not necessarily *on* the bottom.

Dragging bottom is no prerequisite for catching walleyes. The only time the sinker must be on the bottom is when you're fishing from shore without a bobber. There are no alternatives here; gravity takes care of that. In this case the sinker should be a slider, through which the line can easily travel when you get a bite. The sinker creates no stir on the bottom that might spook fish, and it gives the biting walleye a minimum of resistance, so that his suspicion is not aroused. Moreover, regardless of sinker type when shore-fishing on the bottom, the freely swimming minnow cavorts as high as your leader is long. If your minnow is hooked properly it swims above the bottom.

While trolling in shallow water less than ten feet deep, it is usually more productive to let out lots of line. This way your bait is back beyond where the boat might spook the fish. In this instance always use light sinkers, one-half or even one-quarter ounce, so that your line will drag way back, bumping bottom only occasionally, preferably only when you push your rod tip back to check depth. Likewise, when you troll with jigs or deep-running plugs, let out plenty of line, but only enough to get down to the bottom, especially with the plugs. If you have too much line out, the plug will plow a steady furrow through the bottom, mystifying the fish, who is no farmer. You will be snagged more than you wish. With jigs, even with a mile of line out, your constant jigging action pulls it off the bottom regularly. If you were to pull the jig steadily, simply dragging it over the bottom, you would catch significantly fewer fish.

When deep water trolling, in water over fifteen feet and sometimes over thirty feet, it is important that you use enough weight to get to the bottom. Some trollers on Lake of the Woods, Winnie, and Mille Lacs use up to four and six ounces of lead to take their lines down. My best advice is to keep these big weights *off* the bottom, dropping them down only to check your depth. On soft bottom types these big sinkers will muddy the water and become covered with muck or grass. On rocks, dragging will get you snagged over and over again.

Once in a while, when trolling over areas of clean *hard* sand, I try "letting 'er drag." That is, if you're off the bottom a foot or two on the deep side of a drop-off, don't readjust the line when you get into the shallows. However, this is all right only when the bottom is clean and hard and when the walleyes are cooperative. There is no benefit or advantage in dragging across mud or weedy bottoms or across rocks. Don't use mud and weeds for bait, or disguise your minnow with that stuff — you'll lose many dollars worth of equipment and suffer an unnecessary loss of precious fishing time if you insist on dragging bottom over rock.

This rock talk reminds me of a trip to Lake of the Woods which my brother Steve and I took when I was barely a high school graduate and he was about nine years old. It was late in July and most of the launches were going out to the reefs. Our pilot told us we were about twenty-five miles out when he slowed the boat and dropped his sonar transducer over the side looking for the reef he wanted to fish. There were six of us on the boat, a twenty-six-foot sea skiff, including a seasick angler from Kansas City, Missouri, and two young fellows from Iowa.

The Iowa boys had expensive spinning gear which was too light for trolling in deep water. But their terminal tackle was similar to ours and they should have had an adequate feel of the bottom. Well, they put on a performance that was maddening. They dragged across those rocks all day and were hung up constantly. Someone shouted "Snag!" every five minutes, and we all had to wind in while the driver backed up the boat so they could attempt to loosen sinkers from between the rocks. It cost them at least fifteen dollars for sinkers and spinners, and one guy broke his beautiful fiberglass rod while yanking wildly on a snag. Their foolish idea that you've got to drag bottom for wall-eyes robbed them of equipment and fishing thrills, caused headaches for the launch driver, and cost all of us valuable fishing time.

It makes good sense to remember that keeping the sinker a few inches or a foot off the bottom produces as many or more walleyes, and certainly results in less confusion and expense. Walleyes do stay *near* the bottom, but they look up more than they look down. You're better off being two feet above the bottom than mixed up with the rocks, grass, and debris that are part of it.

As guide Art Barneveld exclaims, "You'd think they were back home cultivating their rutabagas! Do those fishermen honestly think that walleyes want to burrow through a mud flat or a rock pile just to chase a dragger's tackle?"

WALLEYES AND BOTTOM STRUCTURE

With walleye fishing, as with all other angling, the most important factor is location. Where to fish is the basic question. In most walleye lakes and rivers, walleyes are found in different places and at various depths, depending on the time of year, water temperature, wind and light conditions, and abundance of food. Lakes offer several structure types which attract walleyes. These includes slopes and drop-offs associated with shoreline areas; rock bars, ledges, and reefs; mud flats; and sand and gravel bars. In streams, walleye structure takes the form of sand and gravel deposits, often at tributary mouths, along with dams, falls, and shoreline drop-offs.

Except for slopes, drop-offs, and points associated with shorelines, walleye structure can be located in almost any area of a lake. The structures are unique in depth, size, and shape. Contour maps published by state conservation departments and by private sources aid in fishing a lake for the first time. Many bait dealers, resorters, and local old-timers are willing to pass on elementary information about their particular lake's bottom and its hot spots, although good walleye fishermen are characteristically closemouthed and secretive about their successes. With the aid of a sonar unit or a sounding line one can locate the spots on his own. In fact, in the long run your own trial-and-error approach will yield your most intimate knowledge about walleyes and where to catch them.

Of course, a drop-off, reef, or flat is no walleye guarantee, since walleyes bite inconsistently. Moreover, a given structure may be totally devoid of fish at times, sometimes for long periods. The mud flat that produces impressive stringers of walleyes in July might fail on that October trip. Similarly, the shoreline area where limits were taken around the season's opener could be a loser later on in the summer. In some lakes, especially the larger ones, there are seasonal migrations of walleyes which change the nature and location of walleye fishing in those waters as the year progresses. In other lake settings walleyes appear in the same areas the year round. But generally, spring and fall find walleyes in shallower areas, summer prods them into deeper spots, and winter has them more scattered than at other times.

In spring and often again in the fall, walleyes are easily located near the shallow water spawning areas. The spawning grounds are generally in shallow shoreline waters. Typical walleye lakes have at least some shallow stretches along the shore which slope gradually into the lake, then drop off some distance from shore. The drop-off can be abrupt, ten feet or more in a boat length, or more gradual. Along this type of shore slope the bottom is mostly sandy, but often interrupted by deposits of gravel and rock. Depth is generally less than twelve feet inside the drop-off, if there is any such break in the slope.

Shoreline areas produce walleyes in spring for several reasons, most important of which is the walleye's presence in large numbers. Having been drawn there by the spawning urge, walleyes linger in the shallows near shore for two or three weeks after spawning, and sometimes longer. At this time of year walleyes roam the shallows in comfortably cool water, normally less than sixty degrees. Sunlight is less direct on the water at this time, helping to make shallow water living even more tolerable for the walleyes.

Shallow water fishing in spring lures the greatest number of walleye anglers to the lakes. The fish are easily located in these areas, usually near shore, and are often least finicky at this time. Young-of-the-year perch and many potential food fishes are in the egg and fry stages of development, although spawning minnows are occasionally available as food. Because of this shortage of natural food fish, walleyes become more dependent on insects, especially mayfly nymphs, and are willing to gobble up the fisherman's minnow and artificial presentations. At this time of year even the sloppy angler with clumsy gear stands a chance of clobbering fish.

The fact that shallow water fishing in spring finds walleyes with heightened appetites is also related, apparently, to successful spawning. For years walleye anglers have called attention to how walleyes feed like crazy and "bite like hell"

In spring and fall, cool water finds walleyes in shallows near shore, placing dock fishermen on equal footing with boaters.

after spawning. At the same time, however, as pointed out in Part 1 of this book, it is possible that a disrupted spawning run due to stormy or cold weather physiologically upsets walleyes for a time and might even send them scurrying from the usual spring haunts.

Fishing the shore slopes in spring is easy. The location problem is minimal, although some ground might have to be covered before the hungry fish are found. Most anglers use boats for drifting, trolling, and still fishing. Others seek shoreline depths adequate for walleyes within casting distances of docks and harbors.

On calm spring days walleyes are generally caught on the deep side of the shoreline drop-off and along shore slopes deeper than ten feet. The ten-foot mark is offered simply as a guideline. If the water is murky, the fish might be shallower. The same holds true for evening hours. Daytime trolling along the drop-off with minnows, minnow-spinner combinations, and jigs allows the angler to explore his territory as he presents his baits. Calm water is ideal for still fishing and casting jigs from an anchored boat. Care must be taken to locate just outside the drop-off, provided there is a noticeable drop in depth, or over an area of the shore slope likely to produce walleyes.

I've put in countless hours trolling along the sandy stretches of the north shore of Mille Lacs a few miles from my home. Here the bottom slopes gently from shore for a block or two into about eight feet of water, then drops sharply to around fifteen feet. On calm days, especially if it's sunny, I troll along the deep side of the drop-off, following it with either sonar or dummy pole, a rod I stick over the bow of the boat with a six-ounce sinker set for the deeper water. When the tip of the dummy rig starts bouncing I know I'm bumping the drop-off and I steer the boat accordingly. Since I believe in getting out a good distance in back of the boat when fishing in shallow water, particularly when it's quiet, my terminal tackle includes a sinker that seldom weighs much more than an ounce.

Wind alters one's shallow water approach. Waves rolling into a shoreline area or across a shallow structure out in the lake aerate the water and increase its murkiness. Walleyes relish the fresh oxygen and dim light conditions and head for the shallower water. The fishing consequently shifts to inside the drop-offs, further up the shore slopes, and onto the shallower stretches of submerged rock and sand bars. Drifting replaces the trolling method when waves make boat handling difficult. It is common for limits of walleyes to be taken in water less than six feet deep in rugged cloudy weather.

While most walleye lakes have sand-gravel shore slopes, some shorelines are completely boulder-strewn, with the bottom dropping abruptly from shore and drop-offs some distance out in the lake. Lakes of the Arrowhead region of Minnesota and northward across the Canadian Shield are characterized by rocky shores and numerous rock structures further out in the lake. As a rule, a rocky shoreline indicates the presence of rocks on the adjacent lake bottom. Quite frequently, points and irregular rocky shorelines signal interesting bottom structure nearby. Rocky areas near shore are good bets in the spring, and very often the rocks "fall off" into deep spots where walleyes are found the year round.

Walleyes are attracted to rock bars and reefs away from shore. These rock piles range in size from a few yards across to long narrow ridges a mile or more in length, along which schools of walleyes roam between their resting periods in search of food. The shallower areas of rock produce more fish in spring and other cold water seasons, while the deeper structures come to life during hot weather. Winter might find them divided between the shallow and deep places.

Fishing is generally best along the edges of these rock piles, near drop-offs, especially if they're located in water less than fifteen feet. Sometimes walleyes prefer the small rock and gravel that surrounds the main bar. Of course, here too wind and water clarity make a difference. Fish spook less in wavy conditions and brave the shallower areas. If the surface is calm but the water dark and murky, fish might also be taken from the shallower areas of the structure. I remember such conditions on a calm September morning on Lake of the Woods, when friends and I totalled up forty-eight walleyes, most of them caught over rock in less than ten feet of water.

Whether rock bottom types are part of the shore slope or in the form of reefs out in the lake, they harbor young perch and food fish, leeches, insect larvae and nymphs, and crayfish. Walleyes occasionally gorge themselves on crayfish, as do their perch relatives. Jigs are effective at these times, possibly because they simulate the crayfish's darting motions along the rock bottom.

How to fish the rocks depends on the individual. The still fisherman prefers to sound out the bar or rocky area in search of a sharp drop-off or possibly a curve or point along the edge of the rocks. Trolling works satisfactorily when the lake isn't too rough. Drifting becomes unbeatable when the wind blows parallel with the bar, allowing one to concentrate all his attention on fishing rather than on boat handling, since the boat covers the length of the rocks on its own. Obviously, if a rock deposit spans only a few boat lengths, still fishing and casting from an anchored boat are preferable over the drifting and trolling methods.

Rocks present snag problems to everybody, not just to the bottom draggers. Remember that you're fishing within a couple feet of the bottom, frequently checking depth to make sure you're following the bottom contour. It takes just a split second to drop a sinker between two rocks, and it happens to the most attentive angler. Consistent snagging may be avoided by keeping the terminal rig above the rocks except when checking depth, which must be done quickly. As soon as the sinker touches bottom, raise that rod tip! With jigs it's important to keep on jigging. A lazy jigger drags his lead head across the rocks, seldom jigging it, and inevitably becomes snagged.

Whether or not you accept the blame for getting snagged, never jerk on a snagged line forcefully until you've reversed your line of pull. If you're trolling, that means turning the boat around as soon as you realize you're snagged. The first impulse is usually to set the hook when you first feel the snag's resistance, always hoping it's a lunker walleye. There are times when the angler must gamble on these two possibilities — hooking a walleye or wedging his tackle between the rocks.

Most lakes have sand bars, rises in the lake floor, which are sometimes surrounded by softer bottom types. Sand bars can be elevated plateaus or flats covering an acre or more. Other structures locally referred to as sand bars might be ridges only a few feet across and merely a foot or two higher than the surrounding bottom. Whether large or small, sand bottom areas frequently sprout weeds which attract small perch and minnows, which in turn keep walleyes close by.

These weeds are predominantly underwater varieties. However, bull rushes or reeds grow out of the sand, too, and are seen poking a foot or two above the surface. A group of bull rushes jutting out into the lake indicates a point of sand along which one can fish. Such a point, betrayed by the visible rushes, might be connected to a string of deeper bars extending out into the lake. As a rule you can forget about looking for walleyes in the bull rushes. But the weed line where the open water starts signals deeper water, and these drop-off areas outside the weeds are good bets for walleyes.[2]

One August I consistently took walleyes on jigs right outside the weed line in about ten feet of water on Dam Lake in Minnesota's Aitkin County. Dam Lake appears as a small dot on the highway map, and walleyes can be taken just beyond the weed line throughout most of the year, something typical for lakes of that size.

Sand bars associated with river banks are important fishing spots for walleye anglers, especially those who cast out from shore. Deposits of sand and fine gravel accumulate at the insides of bends in the stream and particularly at the mouths of tributary streams. During daylight hours, if water is clear and runs only several feet over the sand bar, walleyes hug the drop-off, occasionally feeding on minnows and other food washed in their directon by the current. At night the fish will move in shallower, chasing minnows on top of the bar.

The river fisherman pays close attention to the height of his stream. He chooses his fishing spots carefully. For example, he might fish at the mouth of a certain creek only when the sand bar is under four to eight feet of water. He fishes there at that time because he can catch walleyes from shore on top of the sand bar, even during daylight hours. When it's shallower there, he gets walleyes only at dusk and after dark. Although this place may be ideal, a spot downstream might be practically unfishable. There, the driveway might be flooded, or perhaps it's too shallow and the entire sand bar is exposed.

As with all other walleye fishing, these river structures have to be tested under various water conditions. Numerous fishing trips usually show a pattern, something the angler can adapt his approach to. He might hope for high water to inundate the bar if he fishes from the bank, waiting for walleyes cruising on top of the bar. With lower river levels he wades through the shallow water covering the bar and casts toward the drop-off at the outer edge. This requires hip boots or waders along with a reliable knowledge of the shape of the bar, perhaps gained by observation during low water times when these bars are often exposed.

While boat fishermen find good luck trolling rivers without paying attention to bottom structure, others hunt for gravel and rock bars in midstream, where they anchor for live bait fishing or casting jigs and plugs. Generally, struc-

Tackle manufacturer Dan Gapen of Big Lake, Minnesota, caught this river walleye on a jig.

ture is as important in rivers as it is in lakes for walleyes and walleye anglers, and perhaps more so.

Most discussions of walleyes and bottom structure neglect mud. Popular stereotypes of this fish rule out anything other than clean bottom types. While walleyes prefer rubble, gravel, sand, and mud for spawning, in that order, and while walleye lakes are "clean," there is a strong case to be made for mud, specifically mud flats in the bigger lakes.

Mud flats are plateaus of muck, scattered randomly across a lake, and surrounded by a harder bottom. These flats vary in size and in shape, some less than an acre in area, others several miles across in large lakes. In lakes such as Mille Lacs in Minnesota, walleyes migrate to the mud flats for extended periods during the summer.

Mille Lacs hosts the world's largest walleye sport fishery. This huge lake is rectangular in shape and covers 132 thousand acres. As many as 15 thousand anglers fish there on the walleye opener in May, and nearly 6 thousand fish houses dot the Mille Lacs ice in winter. Because of its size, huge areas of the lake are seldom fished. Here, at this world-famous walleye haven, virtually all of the fishing is concentrated on the *mud flats* from late June to mid-September. Walleyes are out there during the winter months as well, though shoreline areas are equally productive then. Water over the Mille Lacs flats averages about twenty-five feet. Surprisingly, walleyes are rarely taken in large numbers from the deep water, hard bottom areas between the flats. When fishing, you've got to stay on top or along the edges.

The rich organic bottom materials that constitute a mud flat apparently give rise to all sorts of minute animal and plant life that attract young perch and food fishes common in the walleye's diet. The presence of such food fish undoubtedly draws the walleyes to the flats. Cooler water temperatures, possibly associated with spring action, and greater turbidity of the water, are additional factors causing the annual walleye migrations to these flats.

Walleyes are taken by drifting and trolling across the flats and along their edges. At times the fish concentrate on arms and points of these flats. When fishing on muck, dragging bottom is out. Sinkers are heavy, from 1½-6 ounces, on both three-way and straight rigs. When dragged, they plow furrows through the bottom and cloud things up, muddying up the terminal tackle and discouraging bites. A dragger might have success if his sinker is light and barely gets down there. But at the same time he sacrifices a good feel of the bottom, putting him at a disadvantage right away.

Walleyes generally inhabit deeper water during the summer months. Deep water is cooler, and cold water has the capacity to absorb and hold more oxygen than warm water. Summer is the walleye's peak growth season and they require sufficient oxygen before they feed. Also, deeper water allows less sunlight penetration to bottom areas, creating dark conditions that walleyes enjoy.

In my walleye fishing, I have avoided hunting specifically for deep holes in preference for shore slopes and deep water structure such as rock bars and mud flats. Yet there are excellent anglers who report catching walleyes in water as deep as fifty feet. At certain times of the year they seek out the deep spots rather than a particular structure rising from the bottom. Guide Cliff Riggles at Cass Lake in northern Minnesota enjoys success nearly every fall in the deep places of Pike Bay. Further south, near Brainerd, anglers haul walleyes from "holes" in Gull Lake. These are exceptions, regardless of how impressive the stringers might be. Walleye fishermen seldom find their fish in water deeper than forty feet. In fact, few walleye lakes have holes that deep.

Man-made structures, especially dams and boat harbors, lure walleyes and create interesting fishing opportunities. Harbor fishing is best in spring and fall, with most fish taken at night. Trolling and anchoring techniques below dams on rivers yield beautiful walleyes all year round, but particularly in early spring when they congregate for spawning. The Red Wing dam south of the Twin Cities draws press attention each spring for its fine walleye fishing. And some of the most celebrated walleye fishing in the country occurs in the reservoirs and below-dam waters of the Missouri River in the Dakotas.

Fishing from shore below a dam with minnows and other live bait works for those without boats, as does casting jigs and artificials. Some prefer the shore fishing method to fighting a boat, especially on smaller streams. Dams cause fluctuations in current and water levels, resulting in interesting, changing bottom structure — sand bars, rock deposits, and shoreline shelves which attract walleyes. The river fisherman learns when to fish a given structure in his stream and flexibly adjusts to transformations in existing structure.

Fluctuating water levels in reservoir lakes require careful study by walleye fishermen. Here one deals with extremes. For example, Dale Hollow Reservoir in Tennessee and Kentucky normally reaches maximum water levels (elevation 659) in February and minimum levels (elevation 631) in December. Ideal structure that harbors schools of walleyes at one time might be unfishable in low water times. Conversely, an area that appears high and dry on one occasion will be the hot spot some other time. It's up to the angler to observe the impact of water level on his walleye fishing and to discern seasonal patterns.

A good knowledge of bottom terrain and of the best times to fish the likely spots brings the walleye angler a long way toward that limit catch![3]

JIGGING FOR WALLEYES

Jigging is a style of walleye fishing which mushroomed in popularity during the late 1950s and early 1960s and continues to be effective. This technique is probably the most sporty approach to catching walleyes. Jigs can be cast, trolled, and drifted, either "plain" or tipped with live bait.

South Dakota Department of Game, Fish and Parks

The reservoirs and tail waters associated with Big Bend, Fort Randall, and Oahe dams on the Missouri River in South Dakota provide excellent fishing for fast-growing walleyes. Cars below the Garrison Dam in North Dakota attest to the popularity of this spot on the opening of the walleye season.

Most jigging is done with light tackle, spinning gear, and monofilament line seldom heavier than eight-pound test, with no sinkers or leaders.

Early jigging history apparently is traceable to saltwater origins centuries ago. However, jigging for walleyes is a modern technique, with names like Upperman's Bucktail, Thompson Doll Fly, Bass Buster, Canadian Jig Fly, Super Dude, and Ugly Bug coming on the freshwater scene belatedly, but convincingly.

Jigs catch largemouth and smallmouth bass, northerns, crappies, bluegills, trout, and especially walleyes. Just about anything can be taken on jigs. Bullheads, catfish, carp, and sheephead are among the less receptive fish, yet some fishermen can boast of hooking even these fish on jigs. Overall, the walleye is the jig-fisherman's prime target in Minnesota.

Jigging is fishing with a jig, a lure having a lead head with a "tail" of feathers, hair, nylon, or some other flexible material. In his book *Bait Tail Fishing,* fisherman and lure designer Al Reinfelder defines a jig as "any weighted artificial lure which has *no action of its own when it is moved through the water.* This can be described as *straight action.* Its primary appeal to fish is determined by *the method by which it is worked.*"[4]

It is this method of working a jig that is called jigging. Jigging is the application *by the fisherman* of a particular action to the jig lure. This action varies according to the fish's preference and the fisherman's style.

Jigs come in various colors and color combinations. Their weights run from small panfish-tullibee jigs weighing 1/32 and 1/16 of an ounce, to heavy deep-running jigs weighing an ounce or more. The quarter-ounce jigs are most widely selected for walleyes, but certain conditions might call for lighter or heavier jigs. Because they are weighted, jig lures need no additional lead. Sinkers ruin a jig's action and diminish one's chances for success.

Along with the action applied by the angler and the jig's

Walleye Jigs

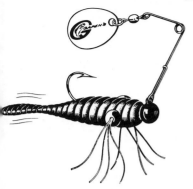

Ugly Bug

Water Wart Plus

Bass Buster maribou jig

Hairy Worm

Barracuda Super Dude

Canadian Jig Fly

Dingo

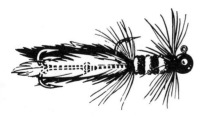

Jig with "trailer hook"

Doll Fly

Bait Tail

color and weight, a jig's effectiveness is determined by shape, tail composition, and eye location. A flat head gives the jig gliding qualities as it pulls through the water. A bullet-shaped head casts more easily and over a greater distance. Some jigs are weighted and shaped so that they will "stand on their heads." Such a jig is Lindy's Dingo.

Some anglers prefer a very flexible tail, one that will quiver at the slightest motion of the jig. Jigs which employ soft-textured maribou tails, the Bass Buster for example, are very active. Various feather jigs like the Canadian Jig Fly and hair jigs like the original Thompson Doll Fly have medium action. Some jigs have stiff tails of nylon or plastic which hardly flutter at all. Others such as Gapen's Hairy Worm and Reinfelder's Bait Tail feature soft rubber and plastic tails imitating worms and eels. Most jig styles have their fans and all can catch fish.

The jig "eye" is the place where you connect the line to the jig. It determines how the jig rides. When the eye is located at the front or nose of the jig, a jerk of the rod tip makes the lure push forward along the line of retrieve. In walleye fishing, the nose-eye jig works best when fished straight down from the boat or through the ice.

Most walleye jigs have offset eyes located on top of the jig head. When casting or trolling offset-eye jigs, the jig rides parallel to the bottom. When an offset-eye jig is jerked, the jig not only moves forward, but its tail flutters. A series of jerks brings the jig forward along the bottom in a hippity-hop style while the tail flutters enticingly.

Essentially, jigging involves allowing the jig, plain or baited, to settle to the bottom, then pulling the rod tip forward to bring the jig off the bottom. The jig is alternately pulled off the bottom and dropped back. Some exaggerate this movement by using long sweeping strokes of the rod. Others barely twitch the jig, using short jerks of the rod tip.

Sometimes, in my observation, the only walleyes caught

South Dakota Department of Game, Fish and Parks

A jig-minnow combination. Note the trailer hook, which helps prevent misses but sometimes discourages bites. A smaller minnow might be more productive than this 4-inch sucker.

were those enticed by a slow retrieve of a baited jig with no jigging at all. On one occasion I was casting with a Blue-tail Fly tipped with a small fathead minnow, tossing the jig into six feet of water in a harbor mouth at night. My action was moderate, using six-inch and one-foot jerks while retrieving my lure. I fished for an hour with no luck and began debating about staying any longer. About that time a car with an old man and a teen-age boy in it pulled up. I decided to stay a while longer.

My newly arrived companions started casting the same minnow-jig combination I was using. Within a few minutes the old man caught a nice walleye, about two pounds. Several casts later he pulled out another one. After he caught four straight walleyes I finally admitted to myself that maybe his lazy straight retrieve was what they wanted. I started to imitate the old man's style, simply tossing the jig out there and reeling it back with no jigging. On my third cast I nailed a hard-fighting six-pounder and quickly followed up with a three-pounder.

Normally, however, a moderate but regular jigging should be practiced. Fish usually strike as the jig is pulled forward off the bottom. However, an alert fisherman sometimes detects a fish grabbing the jig as it settles back to the bottom. In such a case the line behaves a little differently, maybe jerking a little or moving off to one side. The angler should immediately set the hook if he suspects a fish. Sometimes walleyes appear to scoop the jig right off the bottom.

In order to gain most effective results and the most attractive action with jigs, one should use light monofilament line. Six-pound test is heavy enough for walleyes; never go heavier than eight. The drag on your reel and your skill in handling the rod should prevent you from snapping lines on fish. Forget about sinkers, leaders, and swivel-snaps. As with heavy line, these ruin the jig's action and your chances for good fishing. Simply tie the line directly to the jig.

Again, for walleyes the best all-around jig weight is a

quarter-ounce. Deep water or heavy wind might require the three-eighths or half-ounce models. Likewise, if your boat motor rig trolls a little fast, use the heavier jigs. On the other hand, when fishing in shallow water and your casting equipment and wind conditions permit eighth-ounce jigs to go the distance, try them. There is some evidence that finicky walleyes actually prefer the lighter jigs.

Casting jigs from a boat can be deadly when feeding walleyes are schooled up in a particular area and it is therefore worthwhile to stay in one place. Usually it's best to anchor where there is a break, a depth difference, in the bottom structure. Often this is the edge of a rock pile, a drop-off near shore, or the edge of a sand bar. In other situations the bottom offers a gentle slope and one's casting range includes no significant depth difference. That's all right. Walleyes are often thick along shore slopes in spring and fall, especially in the bigger lakes that are characterized by gradual rather than abrupt shoreline drops. But whatever the situation, carefully choose the most likely place. Maybe you or someone else caught fish there earlier. Or maybe you see stringers hanging from nearby boats, with the strung walleyes' tails slowly stirring the water's surface. In any event, avoid dropping anchor on top of someone else's boat or marker can.

The eight-foot to twenty-foot depth range is usually best during midday, although some jig fishermen have taken walleyes in water over forty feet deep in Gull Lake and in Pike Bay of Cass Lake. Early in the morning and in the evening, and certainly at night, shallower water is preferable. When the water is murky, following heavy rains or wind, fish are often in the shallows and less apt to spook. Rough water also seems to produce better shallow water success. Remember that your luck in a given depth of water depends on a variety of factors, including the lake, time of year, time of day, water temperature, water clarity, wave conditions, the walleyes' mood, and more.

Drop anchor gently. Some jig casters heave out lots of anchor rope so that the boat will swing over a wide area. They're looking for good range and are probably fishing over an even bottom. Those anglers who want the boat in a definite position in relation to a certain casting range, or who get irritated by a swinging boat, should secure the rear of the boat with a second anchor. This prevents the boat from swinging around. Anchoring your boat at the transom should be done with caution, especially in rough water. Point the bow of the boat into the waves.

Unless your anchored location is along a drop-off or near snags which require you to gauge your casts, fling the jig out away from the boat as far as possible. Allow it to settle to the bottom. Then, in fairly regular motions, follow these steps:

1. Bring your rod forward, keeping line tight, thus pulling jig ahead and off the bottom several feet or a few inches, depending on what you find best.
2. Drop the jig back to the bottom. Since you just pulled it ahead, slack will develop, so wind in that slack.
3. Pull the jig forward again, letting it settle, and wind in the slack.

Keep doing this until your jig is retrieved, or until you nail a walleye! After a few casts, the jigging motion — pulling jig off bottom and forward, then dropping it, then winding in slack — becomes more automatic. You'll vary your retrieve strokes and develop your own style. And don't forget, there are times when very little action is necessary. Incidentally, when fishing with a plain jig, set the hook at the first feel of a fish.

Casting jigs from shore requires the same technique used in the boat. However, if casting in a stream, cast down-current to prevent the jig from being tumbled into snags. Since the current pulls the jig away from you, you can actually keep jigging without winding in much line. You can jig for quite a while on one cast, slowly working the bottom until the jig returns to you. Sometimes a better approach, though more hazardous because of the danger of snagging, is to cast upstream, then retrieve pulling downstream or perhaps at right angles to the current. This way the jig becomes more visible to feeding walleyes that face upstream or perpendicular to the current.

If the walleye concentration is distributed over a large enough area, you can drift with jigs. When drifting, make sure you remain in the fish-producing area. Often one is tempted to "keep on drifting." If your stay over the bar, reef, or shore slope is limited because of wind direction or range of the good territory, go back upwind and begin another drift as soon as you get past the fish. Sometimes the wind is just right, sweeping the length of a big bar or parallel with shore, allowing one to stay over the fish for long distances. As the old-timers suggest, it is ordinarily to your advantage to toss out a marker if you connect on a walleye or two. However, if the fish are randomly distributed along a considerable distance, don't hesitate to cover the whole area.

Remember that slack line develops when the jig hits bottom. When casting, this slack is wound in after each sweep of the rod. When you drift, much of that slack is taken up by the movement of the boat. If you find too much slack so that you're pulling all line and no jig, wind in a little. If depth and wind velocity remain fairly constant, you can drift along, jigging the whole time, without retrieving the jig.

When you choose to cover the waterfront and there is insufficient wind for drifting, trolling is the answer. Shut your motor down to a slow troll and cast the jig out in back of the boat, paying out enough line for the jig to hit bottom on the return stroke. The amount of line you leave out is determined by depth of water, weight of jig, and boat speed. Sometimes you'll have lots of line out in order to reach bottom.

When you troll, your boat is under power. You can steer the best fish-catching course, not having to worry about drifting out of good waters. Stay where the fish are. Look for them. Use that marker can.

Watch the waves. If she's really rough, and handling the boat gets to be a difficult task, drift or anchor. It's easier for you, and the boat will stop its constant pounding and slapping, something that can be annoying when trolling into the wind.

There are times when walleyes go wild over jig-live bait combinations. Minnows are most commonly used for "tipping" jigs. While the jigging technique remains essentially the same, there are some fine points to keep in mind when using live bait on jigs:

1. Hook minnows behind the lips, coming up from below. It's permissible to penetrate the front of his skull so that he stays on the hook better. Nightcrawlers and leeches are hooked in or near the head so they stretch out and appear lively. Some insist that a worm gob is good. Worm blowers may be used to inflate and enliven crawlers.

2. The jigging motion, especially the forward sweep, should be slower than usual, to prevent jerking the bait off. Also, if fish are striking short, you want to be able to give the fish a few seconds before setting the hook.

3. If your minnow has been badly scratched or torn by a fish, stop being a miser and put on a new one. Check the bait after each strike.

4. If you miss too many fish — "They keep nabbing my minnows" — read the next paragraph well!

You use small fatheads on your jig? Fish are hitting

hard? Fine, nail 'em right away. But if you use larger minnows or if fish consistently strike short, take this advice. At the first hint of a fish — he'll grab the minnow halfway up and hold it — put your rod tip down toward the fish. Even release a little line if the fish runs. This allows the walleye to get a second hold on the minnow, this time with the hook in his mouth. Tighten up *a little*. If he's still there, set the hook.

It's a fact that one loses more fish with baited jigs because there is more length in back of the hook.[5] But many fishermen tip their jigs with bait all the time, and insist that good catches more than outweigh their frustrations.

Color seems to be important in jig fishing, although fishermen disagree as to which colors are best. Apparently this differs from lake to lake and depends on water clarity and sky cover. My preference is white on cloudy days, yellow in sunshine, and black or blue at night. It seems that fluorescent colors are effective, especially during the day. Admittedly, these color preferences are personal; in the long run your color choices will depend on your own fishing experiences.

Can you jig with your old bait-casting outfit? Yes, but put on the light mono line. And if there's no drag on your reel, exercise restraint in winding in walleyes. Let an eager fish run if he wants to, by carefully thumbing the reel. Watch slack line on the reel. Sometimes there's enough space between spool and gear housing to allow the thin line to get inside and tangle. That can be a mess!

Jigs are most effective on sand, gravel, and rock. Jigging over mucky bottoms, even when fish are there, is usually less productive. One pointer here (laugh if you must): After a good strike and after each fish, part the hairs or feathers of the jig's tail. This is for more than mere looks. If the tail is disheveled or if the hairs are pushed to one side, the jig may be out of balance and will pull through the water in a crooked fashion.

In recent years spinners have been mounted on jigs. These jig-spinners are especially good for northerns and bass but they also appeal to walleyes. Despite their somewhat clumsy appearance, they cast with relative ease and seldom tangle.

Jig fishermen always travel with spares. Carry an assortment of sizes and colors. Those small lead heads find their way into crevices between rocks, regardless of how careful you are. And as for walleyes you can never predict what *they* will go for.

LIVE BAIT FISHING FOR WALLEYES

Talented partisans of artificial lures are overwhelmingly snobbish when it comes to live bait. Mention live bait and they see visions of cane poles and bullheads. Bait fishermen can be equally stubborn. Take, for example, Elmer Scheisenwaltz and others who insist that "the only way to catch walleyes is with a plain hook and minnow." Actually, walleyes are caught on hundreds of artificial and live bait rigs. The "best" approach, if there is such a thing, varies with time and place.

With jigs and other artificials, technique is important. Style and speed of retrieve, trolling patterns, choice of color and weight — all are part of the angler's carefully planned lure presentation. The same meticulous labor must characterize the walleye fishing efforts of live bait users. There's more to it than simply tossing out a minnow or stringing on a worm.

Minnows, night crawlers, angleworms, frogs, and leeches, probably in that order, are the popular live baits used to catch walleyes. At a given time or place, however, any one of these might take top honors. These baits are fished "plain" or in combination with spinners, jigs, or plugs. In all cases, whatever the live bait, it should remain as alive as possible on the fisherman's hook. Minnows should swim and worms must wiggle. Hook size, leader length, line test,

Sinker Styles

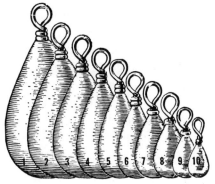

Bell-type sinkers, used with 3-way rigs for trolling

Sliding or "egg" sinkers for bottom fishing and
slow trolling and drifting with plain hook rigs

Bead chain trolling sinker

Bead chain keel sinker

Straight swivel-snap sinker

Lindy "walking" slip
sinker

Split shot for ice fishing
and for still fishing

sinker weight, hooking methods, and trolling speed are also important aspects of live bait fishing.

Before going into the details of fishing with the more popular live baits, it should be pointed out that walleyes occasionally bite on other live specimens. Panfish anglers catch walleyes on tiny grubs and larvae, such as mousies, golden grubs, and wax worms. My brother caught a seven-pound walleye while fishing for tullibees with a tiny ice fly and wax worm combination. Walleyes are taken, though rarely, on salamanders, toads, and tadpoles.

Minnows

Fatheads, shiners, suckers, chubs, and a couple members of the dace minnow family, rainbows and leatherbacks, are the minnows most commonly used for walleyes in the Minnesota area.[6] Preference for a certain type of minnow is most often determined by an angler's experience over the years. Also, in some cases dealers handle only one or two lines of minnows, thus limiting the angler's choice. A few people seine or trap their own minnows, a practice having its advantages for those who have the time and storage facilities required for gathering and keeping minnows.

Seiners take large numbers of lake shiners which spawn in shallow shoreline and harbor areas after ice-out in spring. I use a 25′ x 4′ seine with quarter-inch mesh for covering large areas, and a ten-footer for seining in small creeks or coves where the big seines are too clumsy. My experience on the Minnesota River has been that chubs from tributary creeks are supreme among minnows for walleyes in that river. In the creeks where seining is difficult, local fishermen place traps in a foot or more of water, usually in the deep pockets next to the bank, and camouflage them with grass or roots. Those who do a lot of fishing keep their own backyard minnow tank or pond, complete with a flow of fresh water, spring water if available. Chemically treated water kills minnows.

Shiners are most popular in spring and winter because it's hard to keep them alive in warm weather and because walleyes seem to like them best at these times. Lake shiners are in dealers' tanks almost exclusively during the first several weeks of the walleye season, when they are available for easy seining and keep the best. Silver shiners caught in streams are obtainable the year round. Golden shiners are used mainly in winter time and are first choice among shiner fans for ice fishing. Goldies are the most expensive of the shiner group. Grass shiners are shallower from back to belly, making them more slender than the others and more lively on the hook. Grass shiners are also used chiefly by ice fishermen.

My choice, when I chance it with shiners in the spring, are "lake shiners," or silver shiners, between two and three inches long. These minnows sometimes bear orange-colored marks on their backs, hence the name "saddlebacks." They frequent the shallows of many walleye lakes in spring during their spawning period. In winter I prefer silvers and goldies, if I use shiners at all. Some ice fishermen claim great successes with grass shiners.

In Minnesota, fatheads are the most popular of the walleye minnows in the long run. Wholesale bait dealers trap thousands of gallons of fats from lakes and ponds in western and southern Minnesota. The adults, around two inches long, are sold as walleye bait, while the baby fats are sold as "crappie minnows." These minnows keep well, stay lively when hooked properly, and hold special appeal for walleyes. Most bait dealers in Minnesota handle fatheads throughout the walleye season.

Male or "buck" fatheads are generally larger than the females and become black and sluggish during summer. Walleyes take bucks in summer, but females are better and they are more lively. Unfortunately, since females are often less than two inches long, some wholesalers ship most of the females out of Minnesota, stocking local dealers with males, which die faster both in the tanks and on the hook. This is doubly unfortunate since the females' small size is an advantage in midsummer, when fishermen must compete with a new crop of natural food fish.

The suckers sold to walleye fishermen frequently bear the label "pike sucker." They run from two to six inches long. Anglers who insist on big minnows generally go for the suckers. In some waters, walleyes of all sizes go for bigger bait, and suckers are often the answer. The only way I've been successful with minnows at Round and Okabena lakes near Worthington, Minnesota is by going the big sucker route. Young outdoor writer Don Walsh, Jr. of Stillwater, Minnesota likes big minnows, especially red-tail chubs, up to seven inches long, hooked through the lips on a Lindy Rig set-up.

Least known of the minnows are the leatherbacks and rainbows. These minnows are absolutely the best at times, usually in midsummer, the "slump" period. Leatherbacks are extremely hard to get. While they are found in many streams and lakes of central and northern Minnesota, they are very evasive and seldom seen, except by those who know about them and look for them at the right times and places. Leatherbacks are slender-bodied, the females having a red stripe running the length of their bodies on both sides. This stripe is most pronounced during the spring spawning time. These minnows have very small scales, but they are visible, so they have a smooth, yet scaly, appearance.

Leatherbacks can be seined and trapped, but with maximum difficulty. They don't wait for the seine to hit the water and for waders to splash; they spook when you're twenty feet from the water's edge! Only those who really know their business get leatherbacks. The bother is worth it, though, since fishermen who have enjoyed success with leatherbacks will pay up to two dollars a dozen for them. Leatherbacks seem to produce best when water is warm, starting about the last week in June.

The same holds true for rainbows, which are trapped in the deep ponds and small lakes of northern Minnesota. They are close relatives of the leatherback and share his characteristics, except that the rainbow is more colorful and smooth-skinned. While leatherbacks are most frequently seined in very shallow water, the rainbows are trapped in considerably deeper water. Once in a great while rainbows are offered for sale in bait shops. Like grass shiners and leatherbacks, rainbows are very lively, so lively that dealers must cover their tanks to prevent them from jumping out.

Of all the minnows, fatheads are a good bet for the beginner. Before fishing new territory, however, it's wise to check with local fishermen and bait dealers about minnows and live bait fishing in general.

To fish a minnow correctly, one has to consider his hook and how to use it. For some anglers it's merely a matter of getting the minnow on a hook, any hook, and heaving it out there. In my opinion, hook size and style and how you hook that minnow are the sum and substance of fishing minnows, or any other live bait, for that matter. The method should vary, depending on whether you still fish, drift, or troll, and whether or not you use a spinner. Among those who have rigid ideas about hooks and hooking minnows there are differences of opinion. Here I am speaking for myself and from my experience, most of it with live bait. I believe it is fair to generalize and say that live minnows are essential, except where prohibited by law.

Hooks must be small enough to permit the minnow to swim freely and appear natural. Sinkers should be large enough to get the minnow down near the bottom. When trolling deep at Mille Lacs or Lake of the Woods, this might mean four ounces of lead or more. Still fishing with a bobber in ten feet of water might demand no more than an eighth-ounce split shot. As a rule, use no more weight than is necessary.

Leader material should generally be lighter than twenty-pound test monofilament. I use eight-pound and ten-pound test for trolling, six for still fishing. Some sportsmen use four-pound line for walleyes, a caper which is sporty enough but sometimes costly with the big ones. It's possible to buy good grades of monofilament line, such as Berkley's Trilene, which have relatively small diameter. A small diameter twenty might be equivalent in diameter to a cheaper ten, and it provides "muscle" when using heavy sinkers or fishing in rock. Diameter is as important as line test. The main thing is that leader material be light monofilament line.

Eliminate hardware such as wire leaders and big swivel-snaps. These have no legitimate place in a walleye angler's tackle box, regardless of his techniques. Minnows swimming around with an inch or more of metal protruding from their bodies appear unnatural, provoke fear in fish, and hamper the angler's success.

Following is an outline of my approaches to minnow fishing for walleyes. Some very excellent walleye fishermen may have different preferences. However, they will agree with my emphasis on being careful to present the minnow in a natural way.

Still Fishing

Still fishing is exactly what the term implies. Instead of drifting, trolling, or regular casting, the angler sits himself down to watch a line that is moved only by breeze, current, bait movement, and hungry walleyes. Most still fishermen use bobbers to keep their bait above bottom and signal bites. Ice fishing is still fishing too, and most ice fishermen use bobbers. Bobber rigs yield added distance for the still fisherman because they cast with little trouble and can be drifted about by wind and current. There is a certain mystique about bobber-watching that is able to hold one's attention for hours. Some still fishermen want a direct feel of the fish and angle straight down from boat or pier without bobbers. This bobberless approach is often necessary in deep water.

Hooks

Eagle Claw Aberdeen
light wire hooks for
trolling minnows behind spinners

"Wide bend" hooks for various
types of plain hook fishing

Salmon type hook for plain
hook or Lindy style fishing
with minnows and crawlers;
ideal for crawler harnesses

Kahle horizontal hooks for
bottom fishing, still fishing,
and ice fishing

Swivels and Snaps

Barrel swivel

Barrel swivel-snap

Ball Bearing swivel-snap

3-way swivel
for deep
trolling

Lindy swivel-clip

Bobber and Float Styles

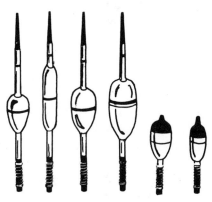

For still fishing I use Kahle or Swedish horizontal hooks. These are the odd looking "big bend" hooks. For regular size minnows, two to three inches, I recommend the no. 6 Kahle, either bronze or gold. Just as I begin to think that gold has its advantages, I catch a limit on the others, so apparently it doesn't make much difference. Sometimes, if the minnow is on the small side, I switch to the smaller no. 8 size. Medium-sized minnows and no. 6 Kahle hooks are my usual still fishing weapons. To prevent spooking a few meticulous anglers use smaller short-shanked hooks.

I hook the minnow under or behind the dorsal fin, just below the back. If the minnow is hooked too deeply it will be crippled and may even die. Before lowering the minnow into the water I make sure it swims freely. If it's in questionable shape it comes off. For weight, a split shot is attached to the line a foot to fifteen inches above the hook. For most still fishing and ice fishing situations, split shot is preferred over clip-on, chain, and bell sinkers. With a sinker or depth finder, the line is set so that the minnow is between a foot and two feet above the bottom. Stay about a foot off the bottom in ten feet or less, and more in deeper water. Adjust the bobber carefully, rechecking the bottom setting. Make sure the bobber stays where you set it. Bobbers should be no larger than needed to keep the minnow from pulling them under. The shot need be no more than the size of a pea, enough to keep the minnow down where he belongs. The walleye should feel no resistance when he bites.

In calm water, some light tackle enthusiasts forget about the bobber and fling the minnow-split shot rig out away from the boat and let it settle to the bottom, retrieving it very slowly, sometimes pausing a few minutes to let the minnow swim on its own. At the first sign of a bite, the line is released, giving the walleye a couple minutes to get the minnow well into his mouth. Then the hook is set. A good substitute for the split shot here is Lindy's "slip shot," a shot with a hole through which the line flows easily when a fish bites. This minimizes the resistance felt by biting walleyes.

In many cases, especially where spinning and spin-cast outfits are used, monofilament line runs throughout the rig and no leader is used. However, if braided lines or lines other than monofilament are employed, or if heavy mono-filament line fills the reel, the hook and shot should be attached to a light monofilament leader of six feet or more.

Many of these still fishing pointers can also be applied to bottom fishing from dock or shore. The sinker arrange-ment is the only difference other than the absence of a bobber. For casting a minnow out from dock or shore, a sliding sinker heavy enough to give good casting distance is necessary. The sinker rests on the bottom while the min-now swims about just above it. When bottom fishing like this, the leader between hook and sinker is two or three feet in length. Sliding sinkers of various types can be pur-chased. Egg sinkers and Lindy weedless slip sinkers are popular sliders. If you get stranded without these, break the pin out of a bell sinker and string your line through that. A swivel-snap or plain swivel serves the dual purpose of holding the sinker at leader's length from the hook and preventing the leader from kinking.

Using the short-shanked hooks, small shot, sliding sinkers, light line, and careful hooking methods gives the minnow considerable freedom and entices leery walleyes. Big long-shanked hooks discourage bites and prevent the minnow from swimming naturally. The same goes for heavy stiff line and wire leaders. There's no need for them and you catch fewer fish on it. My advice is to save the tarpon tackle for tarpon and select gear that's suited for walleyes when you are walleye fishing.

The shore fisherman carefully situates his rod. The reel should be on "release" all the time and some slack line might be good right between the rod guides. Then, if a fish strikes, he can get a several-foot start without feeling anything. As the walleye takes line through the rod guides, feed the line, making sure knots and kinks slide easily through the guides. Make sure the walleye feels nothing. The fish might stop and mouth the bait, and sometimes he'll even drop it and leave! If he goes again, as he probably will, set the hook.

Drifting and Trolling with Plain Hooks

The drifter uses from a quarter-ounce to one ounce of lead or more, depending on water depth and speed of the boat. Sometimes in gusty wind the boat almost sails across the fishing grounds. When this happens you need lots of weight to get down to where you belong. Plain hook leaders require two to four feet of monofilament.

For slow drifting, the minnow can be hooked under and slightly behind the dorsal fin, using a no. 6 Kahle or a hook of similar size. Hooked like this the minnow swims well, provided he isn't dragged along too fast. If a dorsal-hooked minnow twirls, it means you are going through the water too fast.

When you're drifting faster, it's better to hook the minnow in back of the lips, coming up from below, or carefully through the mouth and out the gill, without damaging it. When minnows are hooked like this they pull forward through the water the way they'd normally swim. They are free to dart ahead and to the side, really tempting the walleyes.

When minnows are hooked in the mouth, remember that most of the minnow trails *behind the hook*. This means that you must give the fish extra time to get the hook in his mouth. With Lindy Rigs or other sliding sinker outfits, it is easy for the fish to take line, right through the sinker. Since he won't have to drag a sinker across the ridges, rocks, and weeds on the bottom, the walleye feels little or no resistance. Regardless of the sinker rig, when a minnow is hooked in the mouth the walleye must be able to "take it" for a few

Opening day Minnesota fishermen trolling on Pelican Lake.

Always net a walleye head first; never chase one from behind.

seconds before the hook is set. At the first sign of a bite, give him line to prevent spooking him.

Trollers fish plain minnows in much the same way. If they're moving fast, they'll have to use more line or more weight to reach bottom. Trolling too fast with plain minnows, as with any walleye rig, diminishes success. Minnows twirl and are dragged to death. If your boat motor rig trolls too fast, drift when at all possible, or still fish with minnows or jigs. More and more walleye fishermen with big motors are licking the speed problem by "back trolling," trolling in reverse. This slows the boat and keeps lines away from the prop. In choppy water back trolling invites water over the transom, so be careful. Drifting is the best alternative when the lake is rough.

Minnows and Spinners

The spinner-minnow area of walleye fishing has changed considerably over the past fifteen years or so. When I was a young walleye fisherman in the 1950s, favorite spinners were the June-Bug, Prescott, Free-Spin, and Strip-on types, featuring a rather large and sometimes clumsy blade mounted on a shank of wire between one-half and three feet long. These spinners come with large long-shanked hooks, making it nearly impossible to keep the impaled minnow alive for long. Little care was given to hooking minnows, as I recall. They were strung on carelessly through the mouth, out the gill, and then maybe in the belly. When pulled through the water, the spinner blade would spin and the minnow would twirl and spin around in a most unnatural fashion.

The more meticulous walleye fishermen used to replace those big hooks with smaller, thinner, aberdeen-style hooks. Compared to what I use today, even those aberdeens were large, no. 3 and no. 4. Most often I used the Prescott spinner, Pike hook no. 2, with an aberdeen hook. I soon learned that with these lighter, thinner hooks, it was possible to hook a minnow carefully through the mouth, out a gill (without damaging those little gill rakers), and *lightly* under the back ahead of the dorsal fin. With the wire and big blade it was still tough to keep the minnow from twirling but the wiry hooks did seem to allow the minnow to ride better and stay alive longer. And we caught more walleyes. I remember switching from the heavy wire spinner types in 1959, when I discovered the smaller True-spin spinner manufactured by the Mille Lacs Manufacturing Company, makers of "Little Joe" tackle. These spinners are still made today and continue to be effective. The spinner blade is of the Indiana style and comes mounted on a very short shank of light wire, only a few inches long. Silver and gold blades of several sizes can be purchased. These spinners come with no hook. The hook of your choice (no. 1 to no. 3 aberdeen, depending on minnow size) neatly attaches to the metal shank with a small spring, a great improvement over the split rings of years past. To these spinners, as with the Prescotts, Free-spins, and Strip-ons, a monofilament leader of ten-pound to fifteen-pound test is added, this leader measuring from three to five feet long.

My switch to the True-spin in 1959 represented a major step forward in my spinner fishing. Here was a much neater rig than I was used to and I welcomed this new emphasis on less wire, less hardware. Now I could use a spinner without sacrificing a natural, free-swimming, upright minnow presentation. As I pulled this rig through the water, I proudly observed the minnow swimming so lively in back of the attractive spinner. This was a good rig, I thought, because the spinner was far from clumsy and my wiry aberdeen hooks allowed me to hook the minnow through mouth-gill-back without killing him. The hook was back far enough to insure easy hooking of the biting fish. This True-spin spinner or similar versions are found on cards in various sizes and blade colors in most tackle shops. Provided you choose a good hook to use with it, the True-spin remains a top-notch spinner for walleyes.

I revolutionized my spinner approach to walleyes, accidentally at that, when I bought my first Little Joe Red Devil spinner in the early 1960s. During a noon hour between launch trips on Mille Lacs, I drove into Garrison to buy some tackle. I saw these new spinners on a rack and was told by the dealer that someone had bought six of them earlier in the day, so I decided to grab a couple myself. That afternoon I asked Bob Borris of Easton if he'd try the one I had unpackaged. He did, and wound up catching a limit of walleyes! Since that time I've relied heavily on Red Devil-type spinners. They employ monofilament line all the way — no wire. Many of them come with aberdeen hooks. The spinner blade is held a short distance above the hook by a series of small beads, most of them fluorescent red in color.

Red Devil Spinners and similar versions come on thirty-pound line to insure maximum use and protect against loss of big fish. If lighter line were used, some careless fishermen would blame the manufacturer for the big ones lost. Also, there is a tendency for the clevices or saddles on which the blades ride to cut into the line. However, those inventive fishermen who are interested in longer leaders and lighter line can dismantle the packaged product and retie it, using leader length and components of his choice.

Sometimes spinner fishermen hook minnows through the lips or through the mouth and out a gill, stopping there. In these cases a shorter-shanked hook is adequate, and again there is the need to "let 'em take it" for a few seconds before setting the hook. This can be done by lowering the rod tip toward the fish and maybe releasing a little line. With the aberdeen hook, which is longer-shanked, the minnow should be mouth-gill-back hooked, but without damaging the gill rakers. Simply hold the rod toward the fish for a few seconds when he bites and set the hook when he seems to have it. With the hook well back on the minnow, there are many times when the fish takes the whole works

Spinners

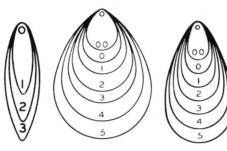

Willowleaf, Colorado, Indiana
spinner blade styles

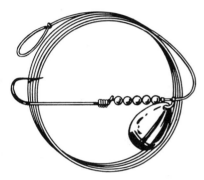

Little Joe Red Devil Spinner
with monofilament leader

True-spin spinner with blade
mounted on short metal shank

June-Bug style spinner
mounted on wire shaft
of various lengths

Crawler harness employing
small Colorado blade

Colorado spinner with treble
hook, often used with
angleworms or crawler

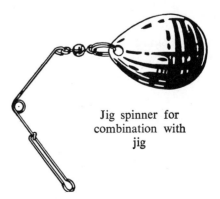

Jig spinner for
combination with
jig

right away. While guiding, I've had countless walleyes "hang themselves" on my pole in the holder when I'm at the opposite end of the boat helping another fisherman.

Spinner blade size makes a difference, as does blade style. A size 3 blade is generally the best for walleyes, although smaller ones are good, especially when fish are touchy. Indiana and Colorado blade styles are most popular. These come in smooth and hammered finishes. Silver, brass, gold, and a variety of fluorescent colors decorate the blades.

As with jigs and artificials, color is a matter of personal choice and often depends on sky cover, water clarity, and the temperament of walleyes in a given lake. I favor silver on cloudy days and brass or gold when it's sunny. If I spent as much time pulling silver or other colors when I usually use gold, I'd probably catch as many fish and maybe more on some days. I was taught a useful lesson on a sunny day at Lake of the Woods. During the first hour of our trip, resorter Gary Noble and launch pilot Mike Gomache out-fished me and the others on the boat. I was using a gold spinner. Gary and Mike showed us how they used green fluorescent spinners. After the rest of us switched, our luck evened out.

Spinners are drifted and trolled. Still fishermen seldom find spinners to their advantage. When to use spinners in place of plain hook outfits is difficult to pinpoint. There are definitely times when each is superior by far. Trial-and-error experience gives you the answers.

Crawlers and Angleworms

Night crawlers are often the solution to midsummer walleye fishing problems. With some exceptions, early spring, autumn, and winter are the poorest times for crawler fishing. I seldom use worms before the first week of June and after the first week in October. When most walleye fishermen talk about "worms" they mean night crawlers, not the smaller angleworms. But the smaller ones should be included in this discussion of worms because they do catch walleyes, sometimes better than the big juicy night crawlers.

Ordinarily angleworms are in great supply in the nearest garden. Rich organic soil that has been worked and watered is ideal, as are the damp lower reaches of leaf and mulch piles. Angleworms and night crawlers prefer cool moist surroundings. Use a fork for digging worms, since shovels cut too many worms into pieces. Hunt for crawlers at night on lawns after sprinkling or a rain shower. At night, if it's damp enough, the crawlers stretch out just outside their holes. Footsteps and bright light send the quick worms into those holes before you even see them. Crawlers are least cautious during the rain.

Proceeding very quietly on hands and knees, the crawler hunter should use a dim flashlight, watching the barely visible ground just ahead of the main light beam. Grab crawlers *before* the light is shined directly at them. If a crawler has already started into his hole by the time you get a hold on him, slowly ease him out. Impatient pulling tears crawlers in half.

Crawlers team up with plain hook rigs, spinners, worm harnesses, and plugs to catch walleyes. For slow trolling and drifting, plain hook fishermen hook crawlers in two ways. Some catch the worm in the nose end, burying the barb of the hook. This makes the rig virtually weedless, provided the hook is small like those used on Lindy crawler rigs. When hooked in the head, most of the crawler's length trails in back of the hook. That's why it's important to carefully watch for the first sign of a bite. As soon as you detect a fish, release line, making sure the walleye can run freely without feeling anything. After he's taken between twelve and fifteen feet of line, meaning he's had some time to mouth the crawler, set the hook.

Other plain hookers impale the worm once in his reproduction ring, sometimes catching him a second time further back. Generally, the old idea of "weaving" a worm onto the hook, a practice common among bullhead and panfish anglers, is shunned by good walleye fishermen.

When plain-hooking angleworms, use four or five good-sized ones, more if they're small, hooking each one no more than twice. This gives you a genuine wiggling "gob o' worms."

Crawlers are good behind spinners. Once in a while you'll run across a walleye hound, usually an old-timer, who replaces the single hook with a treble in back of the spinner. This is unnecessary. The same spinners used with minnows, with the same hooks, are adequate. I hook the crawler twice, once in the reproduction ring, and once back a little farther, leaving a couple inches to trail. Sometimes two juicy crawlers are enticing.

In recent years special worm-spinner outfits called "worm harnesses" have dominated the spinner method of fishing walleyes with crawlers. The harness is a special worm leader consisting of several feet of monofilament leader, a spinner blade, beads, and two or three hooks about two inches apart. The worm is hooked in the head, in the middle, and toward the posterior if there are three hooks. The angler has the advantage of the spinner, a stretched-out worm (instead of a gob), and several sharp hooks in place of one.

Most worm harnesses feature fluorescent spinner blades, especially red, orange, green, and blue. Some fishermen lean toward the metallic colors and also toward blades fashioned from imitation pearl. Indiana and Colorado types prevail, although some harnesses come equipped with propeller and teardrop-style blades.

Another effective way of using crawlers and angleworms for walleyes is to troll or drift with plug-worm combinations. The crawler or gob of angleworms are hooked on the back treble hook of various plugs, especially Flatfish, Brooks Reefers, and Lazy Ikes. One or two crawlers can be hooked a couple times each. A fishing friend of mine, Erma Barne-

Gordy Danielson of Pequot Lakes, Minnesota, caught his 11 pound, 5 ounce walleye on Whitefish Lake, using a night crawler and Lindy rig. A pop cooler with worm bedding works best for keeping angleworms and crawlers.

veld, uses two or three big crawlers on her "meat pole." The worms are hooked toward the head on an orange Flatfish. To the treble hook Erma affixes a long-shanked trailer hook to help catch the short strikers. Her Flatfish-worm combo adds up to a foot of bait!

The X4 and X5 models are most popular in the Flatfish line. The middle hooks are removed to avoid tangles in the landing net. And with the middle hooks removed, the lure wobbles more, really making that worm work. Orange and yellow are reliable colors, but just about any color will work. I've seen walleyes up to seven pounds taken on the "frog" color and limits of hefty ones yanked home on silver Flatfish. In the Leech Lake area the Brooks Reefer, a jointed plastic lure, is popular with worm fishermen, especially when the going gets tough in August.

Most worm enthusiasts are very partisan in support of their own particular method. Harness fishermen think their approach is best. Plain hook partisans argue that harnesses and plugs are unnatural, too much hardware. Plug fishermen think their setup has more fish-attracting "action." Actually, all three of these approaches to fooling walleyes with worms can be equally effective and ineffective.

Perhaps there's truth to contentions that crawler-caught walleyes are bigger than the general run. I can say with a fair amount of confidence that Flatfish and worms produce more walleyes over three pounds at Mille Lacs than do most rigs. Likewise, Marv Koep's Nisswa Bait Shop produces piles of photos of lunker walleyes taken from Whitefish, Gull, and neighboring central Minnesota lakes caught on Lindy Rig-crawler combinations. Maybe the worm boys have something on the size bit. It's hard to say for sure. After all, what is "sure" about walleyes?

It sounds funny, but tackle dealers sell worm blowers for crawler fishermen. That's right, these plastic bottles equipped with needles are inserted in the crawler's reproduction band and squeezed to inflate the worm. Inflated worms stay slightly off the bottom, ideal for plain hook bottom rigs. The blown-up worms appear more lively. In fact, even those lazy half-dead crawlers quickly come to life with a couple squeezes of the worm blower.

Night crawlers and angleworms can be purchased at most bait shops. Wholesale dealers pack the worms in moist bedding, a paper product that is clean on the fingers and loved by the worms. The worms come in cartons of a dozen or eighteen crawlers and several dozen angleworms.

Frogs and Leeches

When outdoor writers give listings of baits used for walleyes, frogs wind up near the bottom and leeches are often neglected entirely. This neglect arises from the fact that frogs and leeches are indeed used infrequently by walleye fishermen. It is understandable that writers should neglect an unpopular bait, but it is misleading. Year after year some of the finest fall catches of walleyes are made on frogs. Impressive summer stringers are taken on leeches. Availability is a problem with both these baits, which are regarded even by their users as "seasonal." Perhaps that is why they are generally unpopular and receive scant attention, even though they catch walleyes.

Frogs are most often associated with fall fishing, especially night fishing from shore. Smaller frogs are preferred, and for some reason, maybe the fish's preference, green ones are chosen over the brown ones. Most shore fishermen and trollers hook frogs behind the lips. The former sometimes hook the frog in one thigh, giving him plenty of freedom. When a bobber is used, sinkers must be heavier than those used with minnows, since the frog tends to float and swim his way toward the surface. At least a quarter-ounce of lead is desirable for bobber fishing.

In autumn there is a migration of frogs from surrounding areas into the lakes. Some anglers theorize that walleyes, already more comfortable in shallow water because of the colder water, cruise the shoreline areas especially at night devouring the newly arriving frogs. Whether they're there because of the frogs or not, walleyes do go for frog on the hook.

Frogs can be trolled behind spinners, and they sometimes produce in deep water during the daytime, even in midsummer. This is the time of year when leeches are in vogue among anglers in some places. A bait dealer in Minnesota's Ottertail region sells more leeches than night crawlers. The same holds true at Leech Lake. On the other hand, a resorter at Cass Lake claims he's never heard of using leeches for walleyes.

Generally, the leeches are fished like crawlers, on plain hooks and on spinners. Few fishermen use them on plugs. I have had my best fishing with leeches by hooking medium-sized ones through the big sucker end once, using a small single hook on a three-foot leader. The only die-hard leech fisherman of my acquaintance is Charlie Yates of Hamel, Minnesota, a tiny community west of the Twin Cities. I've watched him make great catches on leeches, like the time he and a friend doubled on walleyes at least four times in between their numerous singles. That was a hot calm afternoon in deep water at Mille Lacs during the last of June, when many of the walleyes had moved out to the flats. Charlie and his partner have experienced very good luck on nice walleyes with leeches. Admittedly, he has also suffered embarrassing "skunkings" with his leeches, while others caught fish, suggesting that leeches, like frogs, are baits for the moment, more so than minnows or crawlers. Even so, I've seen launches at Leech Lake, Minnesota haul in walleyes for weeks on end using leeches exclusively.

WALLEYES AND ARTIFICIALS

Walleyes strike artificial lures and spoons. These are less popular among walleye fishermen than among bass and northern pike anglers, but they do catch walleyes. There are some places where artificial lures are used for walleyes only at dusk and at night. In other areas casters toss plugs day and night. Many fishermen are content to allow plugs a back seat position in their walleye tackle arsenal. They point to times when plugs fail right in the middle of excellent live bait fishing. Yet there are skilled anglers who catch nearly all their walleyes on plugs. And there are those, like myself, who use them mainly around sundown and clobber fish on them "once in a while."

While walleyes bite on a variety of plugs, sinking and diving models worked just above the bottom produce the most fish. Only rarely do walleyes mouth surface plugs. Since artificials are widely fished in water less than twelve feet deep and often shallower, especially at night, sinkers must be light if used at all. Ordinarily one or two split shot about eighteen inches from the lure are adequate, provided any weight is needed. Before attaching sinkers, test the lure without weight in the depth of water you intend to fish. If it bumps bottom, even occasionally, use no lead whatever. This test should be conducted when trolling with forty or fifty yards of line out.

Until recent years it was fashionable for walleye fishermen to use a wire leader with any plug because of the possibility of tangling with a northern, a line-cutting customer if there ever was one. Also, as a respected writer of fishing literature pointed out in his book of the late 1940s, "There are definite advantages in having a leader on a casting line. The bait casting leader facilitates the changing of lures and saves the line from raking against the sharp outer edges of a rocky recess."[7]

If leaders gave the fisherman protection from some hazards, they also discouraged bites by spooking fish and by interfering with normal lure action. That is why, today, it is desirable to entirely neglect wire and nylon leaders when walleye fishing. If a lure man is worried about his line twisting from a lure's wobbling action he may resort to a swivel-snap, a small one to be sure, but no old-fashioned leaders. If you are in the minority of walleye lure draggers who use the heavy braided casting line, then make your own "leader" from light monofilament line.

Walleyes are taken on River Runts, Pikie Minnows, Bass-O-Renos, and Red Eye Wigglers. During his guiding days, retired tackle promoter and long-time fisherman Gene Shapinski caught many of his walleyes on Cisco Kid lures. When I was a lad of ten, my dad did a little night trolling and caught walleyes on the L & S Bassmaster. My neighbor Bob Pieper has taken limits on L & S Mirrolures and Pan-masters. In 1969 the Garrison Walleye Festival contest was won by a northern pike angler who caught a ten-pound walleye "by accident" on a Daredevle. Hundreds of kinds of lures take walleyes.

During the 1950s the Lazy Ike became extremely popular throughout the Minnesota region, and it continues to be an effective artificial today. Ikes come in a fantastic array of colors, from black to banana. In the 1960s the rage became the Original Floating Rapala, created by Lauri Rapala and sons of Finland. These lures are crafted in Finland and distributed by the Normark Corporation of Minneapolis. Rapalas are designed to simulate a swimming minnow and come in a variety of floating and sinking models. I use Ikes, Rapalas, and other artificial lures almost exclusively at night, simply because I enjoy using live bait during the daytime. Admittedly, I have watched limits of walleyes being landed on artificials at high noon, right next to me.

Plugs are more frequently trolled than cast, although casting is quite popular along the rivers. Trolling plugs for walleyes requires a slow-idling motor. Usually "a mile" of line is let out in back of the boat, so that the lure is more than a hundred feet behind the motor. It should ride just above the bottom, bumping occasionally. If it constantly drags, wind in a little line, or troll a little slower. It's some-

Popular Walleye Lures

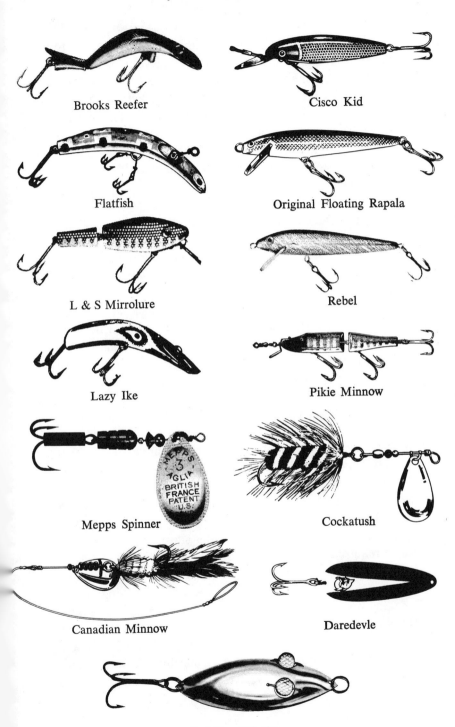

Brooks Reefer

Cisco Kid

Flatfish

Original Floating Rapala

L & S Mirrolure

Rebel

Lazy Ike

Pikie Minnow

Mepps Spinner

Cockatush

Canadian Minnow

Daredevle

Red Eye Wiggler

times wise to vary one's speed, within the slow range, to discover what speed is best for your lure, your depth, and the fish you're facing. Drop-off and slope areas outside the weed beds near shore are good trolling bets, as are the larger bars and reefs, provided they are in less than twenty feet of water. In some of the big lakes the shoreline areas are nearly devoid of walleyes during the summer months, and the deeper flats and bars are sometimes ill-suited for plugs, trolled or cast.

Trolling at night is intriguing and downright romantic. A quiet starlit night on the lake is often a vacation highlight. During the first several weeks of the season I fish this way, usually by myself after a day's guiding. It's relaxing and I'm often rewarded with nice catches of walleyes.

Opening Day midnighters often drag plugs. With the approach of the magic hour, hundreds of dock and launching areas bustle with activity. Outboards are warmed up, tackle is checked, and after impatient glances at the watch, fishermen steer their boats for the shallow water walleye haunts. Through the darkness one can hear the characteristic hum of idling motors and muffled voices, once in a while a shout of "I got him!"

Most of the night trolling for walleyes is done in from four to ten feet of water in shoreline areas. Fishermen usually leave the dock about an hour before sundown and fish until a few hours after dark; some stay longer. Before joining the ranks of nocturnal trollers you should have a good idea of depth, type of bottom, and shoreline where you fish. Remember where your landing site is, and be sure to have required lighting on the boat.

After idling the motor down to a slow troll, drop the lure into the water and pull it at the normal fishing speed, making sure it is untangled. Check its action and notice how the rod tip acts. A lure that really wobbles will make your rod tip vibrate constantly as the lure is trolled. A less active lure, such as the Rapala, is hardly felt on the rod,

but its action can be detected by pulling the rod tip forward
at a fast pace — then the vibrations will appear. This observation lets you know how the whole business should
"feel" to you. It'll make it easier to tell when the lure is
tangled or dragging weeds.

After assuring yourself that your lure is tangle-free, let
it out gradually from the boat. When trolling at night remember these pointers:

1. Bring a flashlight for exploring the tackle box,
   landing and unhooking fish, stringing them,
   and untangling line.
2. It's sometimes wise to use a rubber or plastic
   landing net, since plugs tangle less in these
   than they do in the cloth nets. When that walleye thrashes around in the net with two or
   three trebles sticking out of his mouth, it can
   mean a mess.
3. When turning the boat, either wind up the
   lines and then quickly turn, or if you leave
   lines in the water on the turn, make that turn
   wide, since you've got lots of line out there.
   You don't want to run over the lines.
4. The fisherman who handles the motor should
   know where the lines are at all times.
5. Vary your trolling speed and change lures and
   colors if you fail to get action within an hour.
6. Since you're using artificials, set the hook as
   soon as a fish strikes. This applies day and
   night. Minnows and worms have to be in the
   fish's mouth far enough before you set the
   hook. Walleyes sometimes mouth live bait for
   minutes. When trolling with plugs, you either
   have him or you don't, but more often he's
   yours!

Casting is preferred when fishing a limited area, such as
a harbor mouth or a small reef or bar. Shore fishermen

necessarily cast, and river anglers do it all the time, from shore, pier, barge, or anchored boat. Probably river walleyes are more susceptible to artificials because of the murky water conditions typical of most river environments. The lures already mentioned are frequently used, along with others including Sonics. Some folks cast Sonic-type lures across sand bars near creek mouths with good results. They like to have at least four feet of water over the sand. Other casters head for turbulent water below dams and rapids. Snags can be a problem in the river, so bring replacement tackle along.

Walleyes snap at spoons in virgin waters and when they rampage elsewhere, but it doesn't occur often in most fishing spots. Maybe this is because the fish have become conditioned over the years to fear certain baits. Whatever the reason, only a few anglers regularly toss spoons at walleyes these days. If more time were spent at it, surprisingly good fishing might result at times.

Some noble sportsmen pride themselves in going all the way with artificials — no live bait. They say that walleye fishing in this fashion is most challenging and carries with it satisfaction seldom realized by live bait fishermen.

LAUNCH FISHING FOR WALLEYES

Just mention party boat fishing and visions of Florida, groupers, and snappers fog the mind. Yet group fishing from big boats is the "in" thing on several large Minnesota walleye lakes. A growing number of anglers, pros and novices alike, are finding launch fishing comfortable and productive. Families, friends, children, bridge clubs, investment groups, conventioners, senior citizen parties, and other groups frequently charter launches. Sometimes a launch load is "mixed" with small groups and individuals, leading to interesting conversations and new fishing friends. Minnesota fishing launches range in size from twenty-six-foot sea skiffs to seventy-foot party boats that can accommodate an excursion of as many as fifty fishermen.

A fee of from five to eight dollars per person buys guide, boat, bait, gas, and everything one needs for a walleye trip for a half-day. Some skippers furnish fishing rigs free or for a nominal rental fee. Group rates are usually offered for all-day charters. Because the skipper does most of the work, launch fishing is easy and offers even the laziest fisherman an excuse for wetting a line occasionally.

The primary launch-fishing lakes in Minnesota are Leech, Mille Lacs, Winnibigoshish, and Lake of the Woods. These lakes are large and boast tremendous walleye populations. All are in the northern half of Minnesota and are made accessible by major highway systems. Resort towns such as Walker and Federal Dam on Leech, Garrison and Isle on Mille Lacs, Bena on Big Winnie, and Baudette and Warroad on Lake of the Woods offer food, gas, and lodging accommodations, as do the many resorts in the lake areas. Bars and restaurants abound and add "color" and quality to night life in these communities. Each of the launch fishing lakes supports a party boat fishery unique in character and environment.

Leech Lake sprawls across 109,420 acres of north central Minnesota in the Chippewa National Forest. It rests in a beautiful evergreen setting. In fact, one of the most impressive scenes in the land of sky-blue waters is Leech Lake viewed from Highway 371 entering Walker from the south.

Most of Leech Lake's 640-mile meandering shoreline is sandy and shallow, much of it conducive to walleye spawning. Leech Lake is shallow, seldom exceeding twenty feet in depth. Walker Bay harbors a hole about one hundred feet deep. In 1898 the last Indian battle in the United States was fought on Sugar Point of Leech Lake, where United States soldiers were repulsed when they tried to capture the Chippewa Chief Bug-O-Nay-Ge-Shig and bring him to court on federal charges.

Many of the Leech Lake launches dock in the Walker

and Federal Dam areas. Walker, on Highway 371 at the southwest side of the lake, is the largest town on Leech. Federal Dam nestles at the northeast corner of the lake on the Leech Lake River. The launches harbored at Federal Dam are docked on the river. Fishing trips begin with a short ride through the bull rushes up the river before reaching the main lake. Sea skiffs dominate the Leech Lake launch fleets. These boats are modern and fast and frequently travel fifteen miles or more to various fishing grounds. Sucker Bay, Portage Bay, Sugar Point, Bear Island, Agency Bay, and Stony Point are among the familiar hotspots at Leech Lake.

Here, as at the other big lakes, the major emphasis is on walleyes. But at Leech it is fairly common for launch parties to fish especially for northerns and muskies. Launch drivers bear down on muskies during the hot weeks in August, particularly during the annual Leech Lake Musky Derby. During the 1971 derby, thirty-four muskies totalling 685 pounds were taken. The great 1955 "musky rampage" saw many of the big fish taken from launches.

Since most of the Leech Lake fishermen stay in the area for at least a couple days, rather than drive from the Twin Cities or elsewhere for a day's fishing, "early bird" schedules are more common here than at Mille Lacs to the south. Some of the launches depart at 7:00 A.M. They return at noon and leave on afternoon runs at 1:00 or 2:00 P.M. All-day charters remain on the lake through the noon hour until late afternoon. Such all-day fishermen bring coolers with sandwiches and drinks. Some resorts accommodate groups with beverages and box lunches.

Most of the skiffs are in the 24-28 foot range and carry from four to eight passengers. Since walleye fishing is done in shallow water, seldom more than twelve or fifteen feet, relatively light tackle is the rule, many employing spinning gear. Sinkers are seldom heavier than a couple ounces. Straight hook-ups with plain hooks and spinners monopolize the rigging, although plug-night crawler combos pop up, as do jigs and other artificials.

Mille Lacs is the second largest lake wholly within Minnesota's boundaries, trailing only Red Lake in size. This huge lake has a fairly regular shoreline with few bays and coves; it covers approximately 132 thousand acres. Nearly all fishermen that try Mille Lacs are after walleyes. For centuries the Mille Lacs area has been famous for wild rice, maple products, abundant wildlife, and great fishing. Writing in the *Description de la Louisiane* (1683), his New World travelogue, Father Louis Hennepin alluded to the high quality of Mille Lacs fishing much like a contemporary outdoor writer would.

Mille Lacs Lake is only a couple hours away from the Twin Cities. Launch fishermen sometimes drive to Mille Lacs for a day's fishing with plenty of time for the homeward trip. Eager anglers will drive through the early morning darkness to claim their seats on the launch an hour before departure time. Boats generally leave the docks at 8:00 A.M. and 2:00 P.M., although some depart at 3:00 P.M. Charters are available for those who enjoy being on the water all day.

The Mille Lacs launch is large, from thirty to seventy feet long, accommodating between eight and fifty fishermen. The latter total makes for crowded fishing and good skippers take somewhat smaller loads. Many of the Mille Lacs fishing launches are built locally. The Lewandowski father-son team at the Mille Lacs Boat Works south of Garrison, and old Harry Nelson of Isle, are veteran boat builders. Nelson claims to have built over thirty of the big boats. Eddy Silker of Eddy's Launch Service has built a launch a year in recent times, and the Barneveld brothers, Barney and Art, have constructed several sets of the big fishing boats over the years.

During the first month of the season at Mille Lacs, from mid-May to about June 20, the walleyes are found in shoreline areas, often within shouting and even casting distance of the resort docks. Then the fish migrate to various "mud flats," plateaus of mud bottom varying in size and shape, scattered across the lake. During the summer mud flat fishing, launches dominate the fishing scene at Mille Lacs. The open waters far from shore afford no protection from wind and waves, so the big boats are preferred. Another reason they are preferred is that the launch skippers have a good knowledge of the mud flat areas. Navigating by compass and distant shoreline points, the experienced launch driver has a mental image of the big lake's bottom. He acquires his skills only after years of fishing experience, the kind of experience that most "good" anglers never have the chance to get.

During the spring and fall inshore fishing, the Mille Lacs launches fish over depths of from six to twenty feet. On the flats, most fishing is done over twenty to thirty feet of water. This deeper fishing requires heavier tackle, and fishermen are usually instructed to leave spinning gear behind. Deep water trolling tackle includes heavy-duty rod and reel and sinkers weighing up to four and six ounces. Reels are filled with twenty-pound test braided or small-diameter monofilament. Leader material is often lighter. Spinner outfits, plain hook rigs, worm harnesses, and Flatfish-worm combinations are the usual terminal tackle on the Mille Lacs launches. While most launches employ straight set-ups, some resorters outfit their guests with three-way rigs, using bell sinkers and extra long leaders.

Winnibigoshish is one of the outstanding walleye lakes of Minnesota and the north country. "Big Winnie" joins Cutfoot Sioux Lake and the two lakes are part of the headwaters of the Mississippi River. In the lumbering days huge rafts of logs were floated across Winnie on their way to the mills. Most of the surrounding area is in the Chippewa National Forest where hundreds of forested acres provide havens for deer and partridge. Lake Winnibigoshish is north

Group fishing on party boats or "launches" combines comfort, mobility, big lake atmosphere, and the advantages of fishing with an experienced guide.

of Leech Lake in Cass and Itasca counties. Much of the shoreline is unsettled and unspoiled.

Each spring a sizable walleye spawning run occurs from Winnie into Big and Little Cutfoot Sioux lakes. The Minnesota Section of Fisheries has operated a spawn-taking station at the Little Cutfoot outlet since 1924. Fairly complete records on the walleye catch in the trap there date back to 1942. Since then the catch per trap day of spawning walleyes at Cutfoot has remained stable, even though fishing pressure on these walleyes has increased five to six times.

A number of resorts and fishing camps offer launch service at Winnie. Daily trips are made to the favorite walleye haunts, including Bena Bar, Sugar Point, Ravens Point, and Bena Flats. Bena is the small town at the south end of the lake. Many of the launches used on Big Winnie are metal-hulled and have been in service for years. Some resorters use sea skiffs and converted cabin cruisers rebuilt to give fishing parties the room they need. Straight hook-ups with the standard walleye tackle are commonplace. Launch skippers are equipped with sets of big cane poles to be used with sucker minnows for northern pike. But here, as at the other big lakes, launch fishing is primarily for walleyes.

The farthest north of the launch fishing centers is Lake of the Woods, a lake that Minnesota shares with two Canadian provinces, Manitoba and Ontario. This immense lake, covering more than two thousand square miles, is the most northerly lake in the United States. Over fourteen thousand islands dot this huge watery expanse, which has upwards of seven thousand miles of shoreline. Much of the island country lies in the northern and eastern stretches of the lake. This area is typical of much of the Minnesota-Canadian border country, with evergreen forests and granite outcroppings. The south and west portions of the lake are open water with shorelines of sand and bog. Baudette and Warroad, the launch fishing capitals at Lake of the Woods, are towns numbering about fifteen hundred citizens. Here, hockey, snowmobiles, and walleye fishing make the biggest headlines.

Baudette is near the southeast corner of Lake of the Woods, about fourteen miles up the Rainy River. The stretch from Baudette to the river's mouth is sometimes called "Resort Row." Numerous fishing camps provide everything an angler needs. Launches are of the sea skiff variety. In spring and fall good walleye catches come from shoreline areas and from Curry, Pine, and Sable Islands near the Rainy River entrance. At these times limits can be taken from the river itself. Heavy launch and small boat concentrations appear in sheltered waters near Lighthouse and Morris Point gaps. During the summer months launches travel twenty and thirty miles to rock reefs in the open lake and up into the islands.

Warroad on the southwest shore of Lake of the Woods offers the same big water atmosphere. Fishing forays range to favorite shoreline and deep water spots, sometimes yielding over a hundred walleyes on a single run. Areas near Buffalo Point, Stony Point, Buffalo Weed Bed, and Gull Rock Reef produce limit catches for many. Of course, most launch drivers have a few pet spots which seldom crop up on the maps. Launch fishing at Lake of the Woods means conventional casting and trolling outfits and heavy sinkers. Spinners and minnows catch nearly all the fish.

The vastness of Lake of the Woods is astounding. Fishing there is an adventure long to be remembered. As for the walleyes, most launch services can arrange for trips in both American and Canadian waters, making double limits possible, although this practice is under intense study by conservation officials. Soon, if not already, only one limit will be allowed. Most Lake of the Woods launch trips are for the day. Shore lunches of steaming baked beans and tasty fresh walleye fillets are becoming standard practice.

On the big lakes, launches troll and drift for walleyes.

Launch drivers furnish the landing net and most often net the fish for you. At some places you furnish all the tackle. At others all tackle is provided, including stringers. Some Mille Lacs guides will insist that you leave your own gear home. Most of the big boats are equipped with a "head" for passenger comfort and are required by law to furnish life preservers and fire extinguishers. The pilots are licensed and boats are inspected by state and Coast Guard authorities, depending on jurisdiction.

A few fishermen refuse to fish on launches because of "people piled on like cordwood" and because "they all drag bottom up ahead of me." It's true that the less fish-oriented launch business specializes in overcrowding. Whether there are too many people or not depends largely on the skipper's genuine fishing interests or lack of them. The good launch driver never sacrifices "fishability." He knows that while he might make a few extra bucks on a given run, he will be out money in the long run unless he consistently provides good fishing conditions. If someone fishes in a way that lessens the chances of success for others on board, he will "lay it on the line."

The stereotyped image of launch fishing, consisting of shouting drunks and tangled lines, should never deter a walleye fisherman from enjoying what might be a really fun fishing bonanza. Aside from catching fish, you meet all kinds of fishermen and characters. And more than a few of the big boat drivers are real walleye fishing veterans with stories galore.

ICE FISHING

In Minnesota and Wisconsin the walleye season runs from approximately May 15 through February 15. That includes at least two months of fishing through the ice. In recent years ice fishing for walleyes has attracted a strong army of dedicated anglers who brave not only the weather, but also some hot and determined criticism from those who retreat to their armchairs and slippers before the ice even forms. Perhaps fishermen continue to go after old "marble eye" in the dead of winter for the same reasons they do in the open water season and more. There is great satisfaction in outwitting this elusive finny character — the number one reason for chasing walleyes anytime. In winter there is the added adventure of being on the ice, walking or driving across the very surface of the lake, listening to it creak and rumble as it responds to the freezing process and changes in temperature. The ice fisherman has the mysterious feeling of the invader, the thrill of treading on sacred ground. His footprints and snowmobile tracks on the frozen lakes and rivers mar the snowy blanket under which nature is supposed to "sleep" and gather strength for another summer. Ice fishermen know the beauty of the winter scene from actually being out there as part of it.

The winter angler can play the role of rugged outdoorsman if he chooses. He can hike out to the fishing grounds with a sack of firewood on his back and minnow bucket in hand, listening to the crunching sound of his tracks being formed in the snow. He rigorously chisels a hole through ice that may reach a thickness of three feet or more by February in northern regions. If he has a little fish house, he builds a wood fire and settles back to wait for the afternoon sun to sink lower in the west and for the first bite of the evening walleye flurry.

Ice fishing can be more comfortable than that, and for many people it is. Deluxe gas-heated fish houses now outnumber the old wood-burning models. Bunks, card table, sofa, TV, and wall-to-wall carpeting are only part of the changing scene. The quiet "natural" sounds of the stove and the wind are interrupted by the whining of snowmobiles whisking their riders to the fish houses and by the equally noisy gas-powered ice augers that drill holes through the thick ice in seconds. Even cars can sail across the lake on highways plowed right out to the rental fish houses, where all the boys have to do is get in the house and fish. The heat is on and the holes are cut. This is certainly "ice fishing made easy," yet for those who live in the city it's sometimes the best way to a limit of walleyes.

Fish houses, while not essential, make the whole ice fishing experience livable. They give the owner more than a tackle box to play with. Fish houses of all sizes and colors cluster into villages on the lakes, with plowed roads, coffee shops, and sometimes even power lines. Mille Lacs in central Minnesota hosts between two and six thousand fish houses each winter, depending on weather and ice conditions. Some anglers insist they want to be free to move around and gamble on the weather without a house. Others prefer portable and collapsible houses of canvas and plywood that can be pulled to the fishing spots by hand or on sleds by snowmobile. There are times, though, in wind, snow, and cold, when even the most durable die-hard can't take it outside.

The standard permanent fish house varies in size from the modest one-hole 4′ x 5′ and the 4′ x 6′ two holers, to bulky cabin-size models up to twenty feet long with holes in every corner and some in between. These big houses are usually stored by resorters who are responsible for moving them onto and off the ice and storing them the year round. Some of these shanties are used as fish houses in winter and cabins in summer. Once on the ice, the house is blocked up at least three inches above the ice to prevent freeze-in problems. Many fish house owners attach runners of wood or metal to the bottoms of the houses for easy moving. Others build special sleds, employing runners up to ten inches wide to help keep the house on top of the snow as it's moved from one spot to another.

Old hands at ice fishing know full well that one's choice of building materials should be made with lightness in mind. Exterior plywood no thicker than one-quarter inch is recommended, as are chip board of similar thickness and

Ice fishermen tackle walleyes out in the open or in fish houses.

aluminum sheeting. Ordinarily, framework and platform are constructed of pine, fir, or cedar, the latter being lightest. There is a wide range of heaters and stoves on the market.

Holes are cut with chisels or spuds, an assortment of hand augers, and gas and 12-volt battery-powered augers. All ice fishermen should own a chisel. Aside from being a handy tool for cutting and trimming holes and chopping loose frozen-down fish houses, the chisel works fine for testing ice conditions when the angler ventures onto newly formed or questionable terrain.

Augers have their place in ice fishing, too. They drill quick holes through two feet or more of ice. The man with an auger is more apt to explore and locate new spots. Walleye fishermen choose augers with eight-inch diameters or larger. Dippers, one for scooping ice chips from the hole and one for the minnows, save the fingers from getting cold and wet. Most bait shops and stores displaying tackle sell these items.

Warm clothing is taken for granted by experienced ice fishermen, but newcomers to the sport often forget that being out on a lake for six hours is more rugged than walking to the garage. Even when the trees in the back yard are barely moving, it's often breezy on the open lake. The old-timers claim that multiple layers are better for keeping warm. They recommend several layers of moderate weight rather than one big bulky outfit. The first layer should be a set of thermal or insulated underwear, some sort of "long johns." Fewer clothes are needed under snowmobile suits, the more expensive ones providing comfort even in the coldest sub-zero weather. Footwear varies considerably, but felt liners and wool socks inside boots, even overshoes, are reliable. Extra gloves and mitts are good to have along. Mittens are advantageous for fishing because they can be slipped off easily when you get a bite, and they are warmer than gloves.

My own preference is to walk to the fishing grounds whenever possible, but many anglers drive on snowmobiles and in cars. Both caution and courtesy must be practiced by these drivers. It is difficult for snowmobilers and auto drivers to check ice thickness every few feet. Tragic early winter drownings are annual reminders to keep vehicles off the lakes until safe ice throughout the area of travel is a really sure thing. If you drive your car onto the ice, stay on traveled roads only, since expansion cracks and thin ice are often obscured by drifting snow. River ice is especially dangerous and seldom uniform in thickness. Open spots are numerous. For cars, at least a foot to fifteen inches of ice is recommended, and half that thickness for snowmobiles.

Hole size should seldom be over a foot in diameter. A ten to twelve inch hole is big enough for most walleyes. The common augers cut six and eight inch holes. If you use the same hole several days in a row, chop or drill it out when you notice it getting smaller. Always make sure that jagged ice is trimmed from top and bottom edges of the holes, since either line or bobber might catch on such places, warning a biting walleye that something is wrong.

A depth finder, either a bell sinker or the store-bought clamp-on type, is necessary for checking depth. These fit into the small plastic or metal tackle box that should be part of one's equipment. Big bulky tackle boxes stay home. All the walleye man needs in his winter box is a minimum of tackle, including hooks, split shot, a few jigs, Swedish Pimple, depth finder, bobbers, and maybe some extra line. A hook disgorger is another tackle box item for those who have trouble unhooking walleyes. A five-gallon pail is good for carrying fish and also for sitting on, especially when fishing in the open.

For minnows, the standard bucket works fine. Since minnows stay lively in cold water, you seldom have to worry about changing water. In case minnows do come to the top, a coffee can is fine for dipping water from the lake. Ice chunks and snow contain dissolved oxygen and can be added to the minnow bucket water if fresh water is unavailable. For storing minnows between fishing trips, keep the minnow bucket in a cool place, maybe in the basement or in the back entry, occasionally adding snow. Chemically treated city water kills the minnows. Those owning fish houses can lower a sinking minnow bucket through one of the holes, making sure the rope or chain is held to the middle of the hole to prevent it from freezing to one side, something that requires tricky chiseling later on.

Winter walleyes bite on minnows, especially fatheads and shiners, and strike a variety of jigs and ice spoons. December walleye fishing is often, but not always, better than late winter angling for these fish. Early morning and the hour at sundown are usually best. At these times the walleye is most active on shore slopes and drop-offs in water less than fifteen feet deep. These shallow water morning-evening areas are best early in the ice fishing season. Deeper areas improve as the season progresses. Many anglers fish in the shallows until after New Year's, then move out into deeper water, often between twenty and forty feet. Here morning and evening fishing are still best, but deep water fishermen often have good luck during the middle of the day.

Sunrise and sunset times are best for shallow water early in the season because at these times walleyes move to and from their shallow water feeding areas. The day's fishing action is thus packed into a short time, often a quick but exciting flurry. The fisherman must be on the ball if he expects to capitalize on this prime time. Holes should be cut, tackle tied, and fire built *before* the magic hour arrives. In the long run, time of day is very important for the winter walleye angler, especially during the first several weeks after freeze-up.

The ice fisherman is of necessity going to still fish. Nearly all minnow fishing is executed with plain hook, split shot, and bobber. The still fishing methods described earlier apply here. Light monofilament line under fifteen-pound test is a must for at least six feet above the hook. I use monofilament throughout my ice fishing rigs because it stays limber even in zero weather. Bobber size should be small, just big enough to stay afloat with shot and minnow. I prefer pencil bobbers, both plastic and wooden versions. Big clumsy bobbers signal danger to wary walleyes.

Small short-shanked hooks are the rule. A split shot is pinched onto the line between twelve and fifteen inches above the hook. Wire leaders, big swivel-snaps, gigantic hooks, and trolling sinkers have no place on the ice fisherman's rigging. Remember that the story of the walleye's life is survival, and he fears anything that even remotely suggests danger.

The minnow gets hooked just below the back near the dorsal fin. He is lively when hooked this way, and he exerts a jiggling influence on the bobber, sometimes pulling it down an inch or so. The novice often mistakes this minnow action for a bite. One can sometimes sense a fish's presence by increased minnow action. Many bites are preceded by several minutes of frantic swimming by the minnow.

The key to hooking the walleye is your ability to judge when he has the hook in his mouth. Normally a walleye will grab the bait and slowly run with it, carrying the bobber some distance under the ice away from the hole. Then he will stop and either get a better hold of the minnow or spit it out. If he decides in your favor you'll soon know, because the line will start to pay out once more. This is when you set the hook, when he goes the second time. Sometimes the fish changes directions; after going ten feet following the strike, the line will stop as though the fish has stopped. Suddenly you might see the bobber moving in the opposite direction a few feet right under the hole. When that happens, pull straight up as soon as you see the bobber come by, thus setting the hook.

There are times when the bobber is plunked down a foot or so, staying right in the hole and jerking occasionally. This usually indicates that the fish is holding the minnow, perhaps swallowing it. If the bobber stays there, you can gamble and set the hook or tighten the line a little to provoke the fish into moving. If he does move away with deliberate speed you might do well to suppose he has the hook in his mouth, and clobber him.

Walleyes have been known to plop the bobber and keep running with no hesitation, stripping out twenty-five or thirty feet of line without slowing down. These bites can be too quickly mistaken for northerns. When I get these bites, for example, I picture the fish as having had his mouth open when he bit, and if he wants to keep going after taking thirty feet of line I set the hook. Regardless of how the fish bites, you and I realize that one really never knows for sure when to set the hook. But an experienced walleye fisherman develops that "extra sense" which tells him when to react, and winds up his season with a .500 average or better.

For the most part, conventional rods and reels have no place on the ice fishing scene. Minnow fishermen have reels or homemade spool rigs mounted above the holes in their fish houses, and they employ pegged sticks or spool rigs outside. Actually the stick, which can be stuck in the ice next to the hole, is meant for crappie fishing with minnows, where the bobber goes down a foot or so and the hook is set. The stick can prove to be a hindrance in walleye fishing, where up to twenty or more feet of slack line must be readily available to the fish. I use a fifteen-inch length of 1 x 2, pointed on one end, with a spike driven into it toward the other end. I shove the pointed end into slush, ice chips, or snow next to the hole, the other end extending directly above the hole. On the spike I place the spool of line containing my minnow rig. With this outfit I can feed the fish line with little trouble, and if I'm otherwise occupied he's free to unwind the spool himself with little resistance. The main thing is that the fish can take line freely and as fast as he wants to.

To facilitate the biting walleye's easy getaway, always keep your rigging neat, workable, and ice-free. As soon as a thin film of ice appears on the hole, grab the dipper and skim it off. If the bobber is frozen in when a fish bites, chances are you'll lose your minnow and the fish. To ward off freezing holes, some outside walleye anglers place a coffee can containing lighted charcoal briquets against one side of the hole. Some pour fuel oil or even lighter fluid on the hole to prevent freezing, but this is not advisable since walleyes are seldom attracted to bait stinking from petrol.

Granted, plain live minnows steal the show in winter. But walleyes are also caught on jigs and spoons, plain or tipped with minnows. Certainly the most popular artificial used by walleye fishermen in the wintertime is the Swedish Pimple. Gold, silver, copper, or combinations of these have been the traditionally favored colors. More recently the Bay de Noc people who make the Pimple have graced that spoon with other colors. The Swedish Pimple is jigged about a foot off the bottom with strokes between six inches and a foot, with occasional two-foot sweeps. After every half-dozen strokes or so, pause for several seconds. Fish often strike during this lull in the jigging.

Those who choose to bait the Pimple with minnows generally use one fathead hooked either under the dorsal or behind the lips, or two or three crappie minnows. Some pull the baited Pimple slowly up and down, others jig it more rapidly, nearly everybody stopping for pauses. When tipping with minnows I use a rather large bobber, big enough to keep the medium-sized Pimple off bottom. During the pauses I carefully watch the bobber. If it dances, signalling the frantic efforts of an endangered minnow, I anticipate a bite, or at least a fish's presence.

Swedish Pimples and similar ice spoons, such as Johnson's Lujon, can be fished with a jiggle stick, commonly used for panfish and tullibees. Others prefer something solid like the wooden "Pimple Pole," either purchased or homemade. These spoons will also attract most game fish, panfish, perch, tullibees, and burbot.

A variety of weighted wood and plastic glider jigs can be purchased. The Jigging Rapala is a fish catcher. This lure swims in a circle when jigged up and down, and it is not baited. Regular lead-head jigs, those used with the spinning rods in open water, are good too, especially when fished with minnows. Tipping can be done by hooking the minnow through the lips — the standard procedure for casting, drifting, or trolling — or by hooking him near the dorsal, as for still fishing. My best luck has been with the latter method of hooking, on the small eighth-ounce jigs. With minnows on the jigs, especially the small ones, it's important to let the fish have it a little while before setting the hook. Some anglers use weighted hooks, similar to jigs but less elaborate and having no tail. As with Pimples and jigs, no extra weight is needed. Lead is on the hook right up near the eye. Sometimes this lead gob is painted. Weighted hooks, sometimes carded and carrying brand names, are fished like jigs.

After a fish is hooked he is pulled in by hand at a steady pace. Slack line after the hook is set gives the fish a chance to shake the hook. "Horsing" a fish in can break the line or dislodge the hook from a lightly hooked specimen. So the fisherman's sense of touch should dictate how to handle the fish — when to give him line, when to ease him into the hole. Walleyes should either be grabbed in the hole when they surface, or eased onto the ice or fish house floor, provided that floor is close to the water. Never hoist a fish out of the water with the line, since he may either break your light line or tear off from the hook.

Whether fishing outside or in a fish house, you can put your fish in a bucket as soon as you catch them, covering each one with snow. This prevents the fish from freezing,

Ice Fishing Lures

Swedish Pimple

Jigging Rapala

Flat Diamond Lure

Johnson Lujon

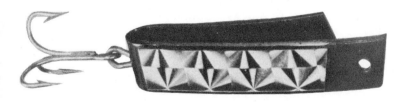

Super Duper Lure

which can make the cleaning job difficult and slimy. On the other hand, some want their fish frozen whole for the trip home. This is recommended if you're not planning on filleting the fish the same day of the catch. Freezing them whole is probably better than partial cleaning methods like gutting and gilling, since these expose the belly cavity to air and bacteria and cause locker burn and loss of quality. In a whole frozen fish the viscera are frozen and kept from penetrating the flesh by membranes lining the belly cavity. Leaving the innards in a frozen fish in no way affects its quality.

Ice fishing for walleyes grew into the big sport that it is during the 1950s and 1960s. Years ago it was something for only the most dedicated die-hards. Now the casual and serious fishermen alike go ice fishing. At Mille Lacs Lake, which hosts more winter walleye anglers than any other lake in the world, there were less than a thousand shelters in January, 1953. In January of 1961 the shelter count exceeded five thousand, a figure that has become near average for each year since. Lower counts occur in years when heavy snow and slush conditions cause thin ice. For example, the winters of 1961-62, 1968-69, and 1969-70 saw snow follow right on the heels of freeze-up, causing the thin ice to sag a little and causing slush to form on top of the ice. In 1969-70, the January count showed less than two thousand fish houses, an eighteen-year low. In the following winter the count was back up to between four and five thousand. The increase in shelters since the early fifties is partly a reflection of an indoor movement of fishermen who used to angle out in the open.

While these figures make it seem like Mille Lacs must be literally covered with fish houses, one must be reminded that this lake covers 132 thousand acres. The houses are concentrated in villages, usually within a couple miles of shore. Large areas of the lake, including most of the mud flats, are never fished in winter. It's possible to look south from a fish house off the north shore and see nothing but snow and ice for miles and miles.

Those who prefer to stay indoors during the winter suspect that ice fishing for walleyes threatens the extinction of that species. Some members of this group clamor for an end to winter angling. There seems to be a misunderstanding about the size and significance of the winter catch that leads to an unjustifiable prejudice against winter fishing and a belief that walleye fishing is generally on the skids. The misunderstanding is worth commenting on.

For one thing, the winter angler has a lower success average per hour of fishing than the summer angler. Winter success in terms of walleyes per hour of fishing has been only about one-fourth the summer success ratio. On the average, winter anglers put in twice as many hours for fewer fish. This may be due to the immobile nature of ice fishing or to the casual approach of many shelter fishermen, some of whom concentrate on "bottle bass" and cards. During the years of official census at Mille Lacs, total numbers and pounds of walleyes taken in winter fell short of summer catches. Also, in summer about 85 percent of the fish caught at Mille Lacs are walleyes, compared to 40 percent in winter.[7] These figures, along with the testimony of resorters and fishermen, would seem to indicate that fewer walleyes are taken in winter than in summer by anglers at Mille Lacs. Only those resorts that "specialize" in winter fishing report more walleyes taken in winter than in summer. Since the reverse is true at Mille Lacs, the winter fishing capital of the walleye range, it is certainly true elsewhere, a fact that should be kept in mind by those who want ice fishing to be closed.

State conservation officials believe that most Minnesota walleye waters contain as many of the prized fish as ever, although some of the smaller lakes have succumbed to fishing pressure. Walleyes are slightly smaller now than they were thirty years ago. Our lakes can hold only so many of a given species of fish before the ecological chain is broken, resulting in shortages of food fish, weakened and disease-prone fish populations, stunting, and the like. Given the same size walleye population today as there was many years ago, it's understandable that somewhat fewer fish are caught. After all, those fish must be shared among many more fishermen. The situation is similar to fishing with a group in one boat: the more lines you hang out there, the lower your average per line will be.One consolation is that despite increased competition for the same or smaller numbers of fish, improved tackle and fishing techniques and serious study by the angler can result in spectacular catches, even today.

To "fish out" a good walleye lake is nearly impossible. Given their type of environment, walleyes reproduce in large numbers. They are elusive; they are moody biters; and because of an abundant natural food supply, they might decline to "offer" good fishing for months on end. To catch them usually demands skill and lots of luck. They live in big lakes and big rivers where high waves, floods, and precarious ice conditions often discourage anglers. Good fishing seasons are often followed by bad ones. Nature herself protects these fish.

If critics are concerned about the numbers of fish being taken and about sharing the fish resource with more fishermen, why criticize only the ice fishermen? Why not cry out against summer angling? After all, this is when walleyes are caught in larger numbers by an army of anglers many times larger than the one that dots the ice. Really, it's foolish to call for blind discrimination against any group of anglers simply because they enjoy doing their thing at a particular time of year. The question to ask should not be, "What effect does winter fishing have on summer fishing?" This question wrongly implies that summer fishing is somehow more sacred, a more justifiable sport. Many of us are year-round anglers, and regardless of what season we choose for our fishing, we should ask this question instead: "Given adequate research and survey data, what conservation measures implemented on year-round or seasonal schedules can give fishermen the best fishing over the greatest part of the year?" My advice to walleye anglers is, "Fish for as many hours as you have time for, winter included!"

CARING FOR THE CATCH

The quality of fish on the table depends on careful handling of the fish from the moment it is caught. Too many anglers blame that "odd fish flavor" on the waters from which the fish were pulled rather than on their own negligence. As with most aspects of fishing, there is disagreement on the handling and preparation of fish. Most anglers prefer to keep fish alive on stringers, in fish baskets, and in live boxes right up to cleaning time. I also suggest this approach because it insures freshness. Some "bleed" their fish by gilling them right away, on the theory that bled flesh has higher quality. Actually, you wind up with little blood in the walleye fillets regardless of how dead or alive the fish is when filleted. It's easy to wash away whatever blood there might be. The healthiest-looking and best-tasting fillet comes from a fish that was alive seconds before the knife work.

Cautious anglers toss freshly caught walleyes into a cooler or box with ice to keep the fish well refrigerated right up until cleaning. This is advantageous when a fishing trip extends for many hours without return to the dock. After a half-day of dragging on stringers, especially in rough water, fish become sluggish and often die. Launch fishermen on all-day runs, especially at Lake of the Woods, ice their fish from the start and seldom use stringers. On the other hand, when the fishing grounds are only a few minutes from home base and the water is quiet, fish can be kept alive on stringers. While the icing method is necessary on longer trips, I suggest avoiding it on short jaunts because the fish die, become slimy, and often assume bent and contorted shapes in the cooler. As for ice fishermen, unless they desire whole frozen fish for the trip home, they fare best by burying fish in the snow, keeping them from freezing, and cleaning them as soon as they return home. Fish are especially slimy after being frozen and the cleaning job is more difficult.

Several types of stringers serve to keep fish alive during the outing. While stringer type makes little difference, some fishermen have strong preferences. When guiding, I prefer rope stringers, especially the nylon and plastic versions, because they hold up to fifteen walleyes each, depending on size, and because one can slide several walleyes down the rope at one time. A disadvantage with the rope is that fish are not held separate from one another. If the top fish on the rope are heavy the bottom ones are pushed together.

Chain stringers with sliding snaps are probably best for keeping fish alive. These are excellent for hanging fish from the dock overnight to be cleaned the following day. Stringers with stationary snaps must be brought into the boat when each fish is strung, causing inconvenience to the fisherman and injury to the fish. Make sure all fish on the stringer are in the water. A fisherman dragging a stringer of fish half out of the water is a sorry sight indeed. This kind of carelessness merits no excuses and inevitably leads to a poor, if not risky, quality of fish eating.

How to clean the walleye depends on the individual and on how he or she plans to cook the finny prize. With walleyes, the most popular method of preparation is filleting for pan and deep frying. Larger fish over four pounds are sometimes dressed for baking; smaller ones are gilled, gutted, scaled, and then fried whole. The important thing is to keep the cleaning operation neat. A skillful butcher can perform his duties without sloshing fillets or dressed fish through a mess of blood and guts. I disagree with those who insist that fish must never be washed because all good flavor disappears with a rinse job. My advice is to wash

The ice fisherman keeps his fish in a bucket of snow inside the fish house or buried outside. Fish are rinsed and filleted with no slimy thawing job necessary.

fish thoroughly in cold water right after cleaning. Fish that are genuinely cleaned are most appetizing.

Filleting is easily learned and can be accomplished in several ways. In the most common method of filleting, the fillet is cut from the fish starting behind the head. The filleter slices right through the rib bones, removing them later. There are anglers who begin by carving down along the backbone and around the rib cage, eventually working the fillet from the carcass. Others begin the operation at the tail instead of in back of the head. The object, however, is to wind up with two complete slabs of meat, one from each side of the fish. When you have only a couple of fish to take care of, and you savor the skin, you can scale the fish before filleting and forget about skinning.

Filleting avoids the mess that usually accompanies fish cleaning. The job can be performed almost anywhere, even on the kitchen table. Always spread out enough newspaper to keep the table clean. Carcasses can be placed in a bucket or at one end of the newspaper to be wrapped up and disposed of later. Fillets should be placed in a bowl or pan of water for rinsing. If you're going to eat the fish within a few days, wrap fish in cellophane or a plastic wrap or bag, keeping them refrigerated. If fish are to be frozen for less than a month, a wrapping of aluminum foil is adequate. For longer periods of freezing, place fish in plastic bags or other containers and fill them with enough water to cover the fish. A knot should be tied in the bags after the air has been forced out, leaving a bag full of fish and water, nothing else. Fish can be frozen for many months, even a year, using this method.

Since the fish are encased in ice, locker burn is almost negligible. Fish frozen this way transport easily with no ice required, provided the cooler is tightly shut. You can cover the fish packs with several layers of newspaper before closing the cooler. Wrapping each package individually adds additional insulation. On long trips, dry ice rather than

How to Fillet a Walleye

1. Make first cut just behind the gills. Slice down to the bone, then, without removing blade, turn it and slice straight along backbone . . .

2. . . . to the tail. Note that the fillet has been cut away from the rest of the fish. After slicing fillet off at tail, turn fish over and repeat procedure on the other side.

3. With both sides removed, you have cut away both fillets without disturbing fish's entrails. This is the neatest and fastest way to prepare fish. Now to finish the fillets . . .

4. Next step is to remove the rib section. Again, a sharp, flexible knife is important to avoid wasting meat. Insert blade close to rib bones and slice entire section away. This should be done before skin is removed to keep waste to a minimum.

5. Removing the skin from each fillet is simply a matter of inserting knife at tail and "cutting" meat from the skin. With the proper knife, like the "Fish 'N Fillet," it's easily done.

6. Here is each fillet, ready for the pan, or freezer. Note there is no waste. Remember not to overwash fillets. This will preserve tasty juices and keep meat in its firm natural state.

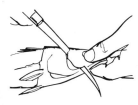

7. Cutting out the "cheeks" is the next important step. Few fishermen know that cheeks are the filet mignon of the fish. Though small, they're tasty and well worth saving.

8. Slice into cheek where indicated then "scoop out" meat with blade, peeling away skin. Repeat on the other side. Many fishermen save cheeks until they have accumulated enough for a real gourmet's delight.

9. Here are all parts of the fish after you've finished. Note fish head, entrails, spine, tail and fins stay intact. This is the neatest way to prepare most game fish and, once you've mastered these few steps, the easiest.

Courtesy of the Normark Corporation, Minneapolis

136

block or cube ice provides sub-freezing temperatures. The fish are already iced in a sense, and more icing contributes to the formation of melted water around the fish and premature thawing, so freezer cans and dry ice are preferable for transporting frozen fish any distance. Always feel free to inquire about ice amounts and packing methods of resorters or attendants from whom you purchase the ice.

Laws relating to transportation of fish vary among the states and Canadian provinces. Some states such as Minnesota permit transportation of fillets across state lines only when packed by a licensed fish packer. One can transport walleye fillets from Ontario, provided a patch of identifying skins is left on each fillet. Always check on these things before the fish are cleaned. If fresh fillets are to make the journey home, wrap them in cellophane or plastic, or in plastic bags, and place them neatly in the cooler. Regular ice may be used, and should be kept in separate metal or plastic containers to prevent the fish from becoming submerged in melted water, which might make them soggy and distasteful.

Fish that are gilled and gutted for baking, broiling, or frying can be wrapped in foil or bagged in plastic for freezing. Glazing whole fish with ice insures longer lasting quality. When keeping whole fish for extended periods, occasionally remove them from the freezer for a quick dip in cold water, immediately returning the fish to the freezer. This renews the ice glaze. Glazing satisfactorily preserves those trophy specimens that you insist on having around for a while to show your friends.

About 55 percent of a walleye in the round or on the hoof is refuse, regardless of how one cleans it. Skeptics point to the "waste" that results from filleting. Actually the careful filleter wastes almost nothing beyond the unusable portions of the fish. The carcass and ribs are ultimately disposed of, whether they reach the garbage can before or after the meal.

A wilderness guide fillets a walleye for lunch.

Walleye is high in protein and low in fat. The protein content is similar to that of beef. Analysis of the flesh shows that in a typical serving of walleye there is 79.7 percent water, 18.6 percent protein, 0.5 percent fat, and 1.4 percent ash. Walleye is ideal for those on low cholesterol diets.

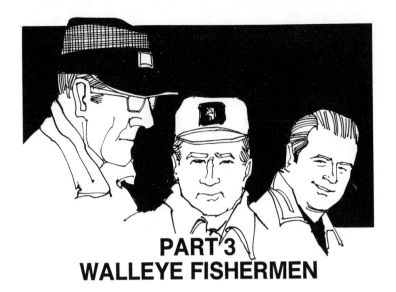

PART 3
WALLEYE FISHERMEN

It is difficult to stereotype walleye fishermen. The spinning artist tossing eighth-ounce jigs on four-pound test monofilament seems far removed from the party boat troller who clings to a stiff-action trolling rod and heavy star-drag reel. The Lindy Riggers drifting slowly over a rock bar out in the lake might scoff at the dock fisherman setting up for an evening of bottom fishing. And it's hard to picture that old couple with their pontoon and cane poles out on the ice in January's zero temperatures.

This diversity among walleye fishermen and their modes of operation illustrates the dynamic quality of walleye fishing. There truly is "something for everybody," and there will always be something beyond today's horizon. Since walleyes inhabit different waters at different times, in a variety of lake and stream situations, they have produced an angling army which is anything but uniform. You might have to go some distance before encountering your ideal walleye fishing partner.

Nevertheless, whether at Lake Oneida, New York, at Horsetooth Reservoir in Colorado, or somewhere in between, walleye fishermen do share a common patience and an enduring perseverance. While they clobber walleyes "as fast as bluegills" sometimes — though rarely, they must admit — the walleye game is cluttered with disappointments and uncertainties. In most walleye waters the limit is a prize seldom taken for granted. Hence, the walleye follower values his successes like few anglers do. A die-hard all the way, he takes his lows philosophically: "They should start any day now."

While approaches to fishing differ, comments like, "Let him have it longer," or "Set the hook," or "What color jig?" can be heard across the walleye range. And regardless of background, walleye fishermen talk a similar language of enthusiasm. A willingness to learn from your own and others' experience, combined with a die-hard spirit, eventually bring some certainty and control to walleye fishing, although it remains a gamble all the time for everyone. The novice may lack that qualified "sense of control" over a situation that some "experts" claim to have, but the unpredictable nature of the walleye plays into the beginner's hands. More than one contest has been won by an amateur who happened to do the right thing for the right fish.

Even the best walleye fishermen live in the past, remembering high points, recalling "first time" and "best time" accomplishments with clear detail about bait, location, people, and weather. They're always eager to talk fishing and to probe the knowledge banks of others for whatever fishing information there might be. The alert walleye fisherman draws from his memory file any clue, any pattern, that might lend more certainty and progress to his present-day fishing.

The three anglers interviewed on the following pages catch walleyes in markedly different ways. Brant "Barney" Barneveld typifies the old party boat skipper on big waters, with a keen memory of his fishing past, a steady faith in live bait, and an unbeatable knowledge of the drop-offs and bars that he trolls. The nature of his business makes him a group fisherman all the time. In contrast, Gearhart Block stands on shore, throwing artificial lures at nighttime walleyes in shallow water. He's concerned about wind, casting distance, and crowds. "Let someone whisper and my mood is shot," he says. Bob McGarry is a river man all the way, thinking water level, current, and boat traffic. Time of day is very important with him, as well as which side of a point to fish.

Despite their diverse fishing backgrounds, Barney, Gearhart, and Bob share the devotion and expertise of accomplished anglers. They speak one language — walleye fishing.

REMINISCENCES OF A MILLE LACS LAUNCH SKIPPER
An Interview with Brant "Barney" Barneveld

Brant Barneveld, known to friends and walleye fishermen as "Barney," helped pioneer the Mille Lacs Lake party boat fishery for walleyes. The tall slender fisherman of Dutch descent and his launches have been landmarks on that big Minnesota lake for decades. Barney and his brother Art steer an independent course to their various fishing grounds, setting the pace for many locals. The Barnevelds troll for walleyes, outfitting their passengers with heavy-duty star drag reels and trolling rods. They are skilled carpenters, boat builders, and experienced woodsmen. It's their approach to launch fishing that brings walleye anglers from all over the country to fish with Barney and Art.

Barney, how did you go about catching walleyes thirty or forty years ago?

Well, we used spoon hooks, a kind of a spinner-feather outfit with a treble hook. They were store-bought jobs and they're still used today, but for northerns. One guy would row and the other would drag the two lines, hand lines. We just tied the heavy line right on there. No leaders or anything. I don't think we knew what a snap was. The line was so heavy I don't s'pose the thing went deep in the water. It was mainly a matter of going out in the evening in shallow water near shore. I don't think they'd bite the thing during the daytime. The same went for the wobblers and plugs we used later — evening fishing.

Then finally people started coming up here with minnows and they fished during the day. That was before winter fishing, you know. I can't date it exactly, but it was somewhere in the 1920s when the tourists started angling on this end of the lake. And whether it was spoon hooks or minnows, the fishing was pretty much done by the Fourth of July because the walleyes had moved out to the mud flats and people never went out there. Everybody kind of gave up by the Fourth because you couldn't catch anything in close. I remember the people who owned our place in the twenties were here on a July Fourth weekend on their vacation, and they rowed for miles up and down the lake trying to get a bite and they didn't get a thing. It's only been since the late thirties that we've been fishing the mud flats in midsummer. Before then it was just spring and fall fishing near shore.

Regarding that tackle, I remember two couples who drove in here with rods and reels, casting lines, and snaps and things. I recall not being able to imagine how they could hold a fish on those wire snaps like we use now. Our gear at that time was strong enough to hold an elephant! You know when we would get a fish on that heavy line we hauled him in — right now! We didn't give him a chance. No matter what size he was. If he was too big and not hooked well, I s'pose he tore loose and got away. But our tackle was strong enough to pull in a cow if we had to. And here they came along with those little wire snaps at the end of their lines. I couldn't see how they would hold a fish. To us, now, if we saw that we'd think it was regular heavy old northern fishing gear, yet at that time to me it looked too flimsy to hold a walleye.

What do you remember about early ice fishing?

Nobody even thought about angling through the ice when

I was a kid around here. It was all spearing. The first recollection I have of guys angling was three guys who undoubtedly winter-fished around the Cities — they were from Minneapolis. They came up here with minnows and fished for two days. The first day they didn't do so good, but the second day they finally located the right depth, or where the walleyes were, and they caught some. They didn't get too many. I believe the limit was eight at that time and they were short of their limit when they went home. I rode down to the Cities with them to buy a car. That was in 1937, and that's the first memory I have of anyone angling through the ice here.

How big were the fish you caught in the twenties and thirties?

The walleyes were mostly two pounds to four pounds. They were all good-sized fish. You didn't get many little ones, but you didn't get any really big ones as we think of 'em now either. You didn't get 'em over five pounds. To verify that you can ask some of the old guys around here who speared for market. Dressed out, the walleyes weighed around a pound and a half. They were so uniform in size they seldom weighed the fish. Some of these old anglers we run into on the launches nowadays talk about catching nothing but five-pound to ten-pound walleyes years ago. They're dreamers. I think we catch more over-sized ones now than we ever did. Of course, we get more small ones, too.

When did you start launch fishing?

Well, I don't know when it really got started on the lower end of the lake. I heard stories from guys who came up to Isle on the railroad to fish on big boats there later on in the summer — which I didn't know about. The first launch fisherman who moved up into this area was this Frank Olson who had been operating out from Garrison. They had been launch fishing from Garrison south for some time already. Olson set up about a mile west of our place in 1936. He had two small launches and I was sucker enough to give him fifty dollars for one of them. You see, his house burned down the winter after he started and in order to get some money he wanted to sell one of his boats.

It was twenty-four feet long and came equipped with a Pontiac six-cylinder engine. There was a lot of iron there, but it wasn't set up for speed. It still plowed along like an old snowplow as it moved through the water. I had a dock out and anchored the boat out in the lake. The lake was so low at that time you could find a place in back of the rock pile to anchor it so it wouldn't get the full blast of the waves.

If I had six passengers on that boat it was about capacity. At that time, the late thirties, I didn't furnish tackle for them like I do now. I lacked decent equipment for myself. It was all fishing with hand lines anyway. Monofilament line and gut leader material came along later. When I started out, you could buy those June-Bug spinners for a dime at the Gambles store at Aitkin, and they were better than the quarter ones that were supposed to be better in quality. The cheap ones were better for catchin' fish because there wasn't quite so much to them, I figure now; they were simpler. Later, around World War II time, we got hold of some plastic leader material, which wasn't too darn good, and switched over to Prescott spinners. Then we got the modern monofilament and started to modernize our spinner rigs to where we are now, with Little Joe-style outfits. By war time nearly everyone had rods and reels, although I still didn't furnish the tackle to the customers.

When did you begin running out to the mud flats — when you first got your launch?

Yes. This Frank Olson was already chugging out to the first

flats and I followed him out there the first summer. I found that flat out from Kamp Difrent and just lived there the first years. I never really explored anywhere else because with that darn boat, you didn't know when you went out if you were gonna get back with it or not.

Do you remember your first launch trip?

Well, as a matter of fact, when I bought that boat, that first spring, I had too many things to tend to myself, with fifteen rowboats to take care of. Bob Kimball was on the scene then, or maybe Ron Honnold, I don't know which one of them. I had one of those guys take the launch out that Opening morning. There was a party that wanted to go out. I had previous notice from them by letter, I guess. Anyway, they took the boat out. They didn't know the first thing about fishing, and for that matter the people didn't either. It was kind of a failure as a fishing trip. All the little boats brought in fish and they didn't catch much of anything. After that, when the Opening rush was over, I settled down to messing with it myself. Of course I didn't have much launch business then because people never knew about me. On Opening Day you could always rent everything out in the way of small boats.

I used that first boat until 1941. I remember the 1941 date on the propeller I bought for the second one, which I built at that time. The second boat wasn't much longer than the first one, but it was wider and had more capacity. It was a full eight feet wide while the old one was less than seven feet wide. That old one wasn't a rock-'n-roller, though; it was nothin' but a tub. Out of the water it didn't look too bad, but in the water it was ridiculous! It plowed right into the waves. That first boat was built to be a sort of runabout speed boat. It was covered over and just had a cockpit in the back that only was about the width of the boat by about eight feet long. Olson had already opened up two doors through there up to a small space in the front of the engine where two people could sit. I took all of that stuff out and made it open except for the bow part, and put a canopy over it. That way we had more room to fish.

That darn boat wasn't even designed with a water pump for cooling the engine when Frank Olson got it. It was supposed to go fast all the time so the speed of the boat could pick up the water and the circulating pump on the engine could put it on through. That was out for a trolling engine, so Olson put a marine water pump on there to cool the engine.

The second launch, the one I built in 1941, I had for a long time. My brother Art ran that in 1952 before his own boat was completed. I built another launch in 1950, a thirty-two-footer, a V-bottom job that could handle about ten customers. The one I'm running now is a thirty-eight-footer, a big wide devil I built in 1960. The pilot house is in the middle toward the front and people can fish all around it. I can line up five people on the transom alone. I've had over twenty fishermen on that thing. You could take way more but it would be crowded fishing.

How has fishing changed over the years?

Well, I don't know. It seems that spring and summer fishing sort of carry a pattern. In those early years it was taken for granted that the fish were gonna bite in the spring. The first one that they didn't bite was in 1941, I believe. Because it was the first spring they failed to bite, everybody was shook up wondering what had happened. A guy by the name of Louis Ice, who had been running launch down the line from us for some years, pulled out then and went to lakes up north. He said the fishing up there was just in its infancy. They were just gettin' started up there, the way he saw it. I guess he was referring to Leech and Winnibigoshish. But he didn't stay up there either.

Anyway, the fishing here was real bad that year. Before then it was a matter of your equipment or the way you fished. It was taken for granted you should catch fish when they were there, although it did vary from day to day and spot to spot. But that first year it was bad — it was really bad. They didn't get very many. I remember some people comin' in here and asking, "Well, how bad is it? Are you gettin' anything?" I'd say, "I've been gettin' about six or seven fish on a trip with the launch." And they were game to go out with that assurance, that maybe we'd get half a dozen. Before that it was even worse. It was possible to go out there and not even get a bite. And that's quite a while ago already!

The way I look at it, during the last thirty years or so, fishing has reached a stage where the balance seesaws one way or the other, depending on hatches and food supply and the fish in the lake to eat it. If the walleyes are hard up for food, they bite like mad and get fished down some. Throw in a good perch hatch and the walleye fishing is slow. I would say that's come about in the last thirty years, starting back in 1941 when they didn't bite. Then we had those conditions and I think since then everything has leveled off pretty much, seesawing back and forth within the same bounds. There are times when everyone gets limits and times when we get totally skunked.

Where did you get minnows years ago? Did you get them yourself?

We had to. There wasn't any minnow man around like now. We got lake shiners in the spring by ourselves just like we do now. After we got into the launch business and had to fish through the summer, that minnow thing was our big problem. I used to go down and beg off a few minnows from Irv Kuschel's wife back there on Holt Lake. He was chasin' around the country trying to get a few minnows while she took care of the kids and the minnow tanks. The minnows they had were usually river-type minnows, chubs of some kind. Fatheads seem to have been unknown in those days. If they were, they were "mud minnows" and nobody liked them.

What kind of weather do you like to fish in?

That varies, depending on where I want to fish. But I'd just as soon have it be sunny and nice. I've had some spectacular fishing, of course, in real bad weather, but for day in and day out fishing we'll do better when the weather is settled and nice. Out on the flats in the summer you're more apt to get fish when it's quiet than when the wind is blowin'.

Describe some of your better launch fishing for walleyes.

If you want to talk about really outstanding fishing, let me tell you about the fall of 1955. That was one of the few falls they really snapped right out here off the rocks. Old Harv and Chris Peterson came on the scene here then. They came from Belmond, Iowa. Anyway, the fishing was spectacular. The limit was still eight then, I think, maybe six already, and you could fill out every evening still fishing off the rocks. You could have the whole boat full of people and you'd have the limit for everybody. Just as fast as you could get a minnow out there, there'd be a walleye to grab it.

One time the Petersons were out there with me. We were anchored. Mrs. Peterson and I bet quarters on each fish. That was a lot of money for her in those days, even if they had more money than they knew what to do with. It was nip and tuck. First she'd be ahead, then I'd be ahead, catching fish. And these were all nice walleyes — big ones.

Can you recall any extraordinary launch runs, trips that stand out in your mind because of storms, fights, or the like?

Barney outfits his fishing guests, baits their hooks, nets and strings fish.

"Yep, he's a pretty nice one."

Grant "Barney" Barneveld readies his boat for a Mille Lacs walleye outing. Barney built this twin-engine party boat.

Well, one unusual circumstance was when we let ourselves get caught in a storm on the Fourth of July weekend, on the afternoon of the third, I believe. That was around 1954, I think, because Art had his launch already. The wind was so strong in that storm, it knocked over pret'near all the trees as it came across the island in Borden Lake, and when it hit the Mille Lacs shore at Malmo it tipped over good healthy trees by the roots.

I stalled around here on shore for twenty minutes waiting for the storm to decide which way it was gonna go. It looked to me like it was gonna go on south. She was brewing up over there in the west over toward Brainerd, snappin' and crackin'. We had had so much static anyway that morning you couldn't hear a weather forecast on the radio. So we went out to the flats, about four miles from home. There must have been half a dozen small boats there along with our two launches.

The storm hit shortly after we started fishing. It was a funny thing. You had these boats, some of them only a few yards away from you. And when it was over you could look all around you and not a boat in sight. You wondered if you were the only survivor. It didn't last more than twenty minutes or so, and then you could see around you again. The waves were still rolling pretty high, out of the west. The wind blew from different directions during the storm itself. It was so strong that our open boat with no top on it just kind of laid over from the wind before the waves came, it was that strong. You could feel a type of suction on the boat, just a-pullin' her over to one side.

We had rented out two of our plywood boats that afternoon, a sixteen-footer to a neighbor kid and some of his friends, and an eighteen-footer to three guys from the Cities. The young ones came over and tried to hang on the side of the launch. I didn't know what they thought they'd accomplish because I had ten people on that small launch already. Finally we took them on board.

The other guys with the bigger boat came over to us and tried the same thing. Well, those boats are pretty heavy. You don't want one of them bangin' against your launch! "Get away," I hollered. "What do you want to do, wreck us all?" So they drifted away. Didn't see 'em again until later. They were out of sight when the storm subsided. And don't you know, even with minnow pails and stuff on board, they came back with that big eighteen-foot boat — I guess they'd drifted darn near over to the east side of the lake — they came back with at least six or eight inches of water in that damn boat. Nobody had made an effort even to try to bail the boat or do anything to save the situation. They just brought all that water back with them. You'd think that afterwards, at least, they would have gotten rid of that water.

We didn't fish out the trip that time. We came home as soon as we could. It was such a mess. We had women along and everybody was scared — people kneeling on the floor praying and everything, and me a-swearin' like a trooper at those other boats, you know. They were apt to wreck us. It was miraculous that everyone got out of it all right. Those small boats had no business out there and I was there with the launch against my better judgment.

Have you bumped into any "character" customers over the years?

Oh, yes! You've got customers like Sam Bellows who's come here for thirty years — good customers. Then there are those who are good customers in a way, but you wonder why you cater to them. Then you get those whom you never forget. I remember there was a couple that used to stay up here at Shannow's Hotel down the line here at Wealthwood. They were older people who came up here quite frequently. They were in the casket business; that must be why they had money. She had diamonds on her fingers as big as rocks.

And she always used to bring her own minnows. That's why I remember her so well. He just came along as kind of a stooge to drive the car and haul her around. She had the money, you could tell that.

Anyway, she'd bring her own minnows, great big old suckers about six inches long. On this one occasion we're fishing out on the mud flats and she's got a fish on. There wasn't any particular alarm. But she had something, so I casually get my landing net and go over to her corner of the boat, walk over to the edge there, and she's just turning away on her reel. It didn't seem unusually heavy, but I looked over the side of the boat and here's a thing layin' there as long as my net handle! I didn't know what to do about it. I took one look at him, and he looked at me, and he decided we'd better part company. And we did exactly that. She had a thirty-pound line on her reel, and when she laid her rod on the side of the boat and clamped down on that reel, the old line just cracked like a rifle! The fish went right to the bottom and didn't slow down a bit. It was a big northern — must have been close to four feet long.

Then one time some wise guy came along. I guess his son or somebody was with him. He's telling all the people on the boat how to fish and everything. He knows all about it. So one bites and he's gonna show them how to handle it. He grabs the pole and sets the hook, making sure everyone's lookin' — and the line breaks. "That must have been a big one," he says. That was that for *that* time. A few days later I'm fishing in the same area, near a marker, and we snag up that same outfit. I know my own stuff when I see it. And do you know what kind of fish was on there? It was a pound-and-a-half perch! He had set his hook so hard that a perch broke the line. And it was good line; it wasn't rotten.

Have you ever really clobbered the walleyes at night?

Yes, I've been out at night with plugs when as soon as you

get your line out there'd be one grabbin' it. Once when we first started using Lazy Ikes, around the late forties, I guess — Kamp Difrent was already started up then — this Murray Gage came down from his place with some other fellows. "Let's go fishin'." So we went and fished out from Kamp Difrent. I don't remember if we were rowing or if we had a motor; I guess we had a motor. Anyway, they had two orange Lazy Ikes and I had one that was some other color. The walleyes didn't like mine. The others were catching fish one after another and I wasn't gettin' 'em. So I put on just an orange Flatfish. And on that particular evening, my Flatfish was even hotter than their Lazy Ikes.

I've never really clobbered fish on plugs during the daytime. I know last spring I was fishin' down on the sand, I believe it was afternoon, and I had caught a limit of them on my pole off the bow already, so I decided to try an artificial bait up there to see if they'd bite that too. I rigged up a long leader and started out with a big Rapala first. It took quite a while to get one on that. Then it got weeds on it and I wasted time that way. Then I found a Rebel, a small one that was a little better eating size. I put on that one and I think I caught three on that before I quit. So they bite on that stuff during the day, but not as fast as on the minnow outfit. I know they were biting that afternoon, because everybody was catchin' fish. It was a day when there was good fishing and that's why I tried it. I wouldn't want to horse around like that otherwise, if we really needed the fish.

What really irritates you out on the lake?

I don't know if we should get into all of that, but one thing that irritates me because it's unnecessary and shouldn't be, is this damn business of people first wearing cowboy boots and then kickin' the side of the boat — bang, bang, bang on the boat. I know darn well that that bangin' affects the fishing, especially for those fishing under the boat. It might

154

not bother those draggin' way out there, but it does under the boat. And yet some kid will sit there drummin' his feet on the side of the boat. Those cowboy boots! When they come on there with those things I have a notion to ask them to take their shoes off.

The same goes for stompin' around on the boat. I've seen too many times when I've had somebody standing in the cabin with me watching that bow line. I'll see a nice bite working on there, you know, and this other person in there with me will see it too. So he'll stomp, stomp, stomp outside and grab the line, and I'll see that pole tip come right back up. I don't begrudge 'em going out there to get the fish. In fact I'll tell 'em that there's one bitin' there and that they should try to get it. But let 'em go stompin' out there and that fish'll let loose almost every time.

You're talented in a number of areas — heavy equipment, carpentry, boat building — why do you fish? You've put in years and years of walleye fishing.

Well, I guess it's like you, maybe. It kind of gets in my blood and I get that urge to go out there in the spring like everybody else. It's something you don't shake, I guess.

GEARHART BLOCK AND HIS LUNKER WALLEYES
An Interview with the Man
Whose Specialty is Ten-Pounders

Gearhart Block lives less than a mile from the walleye "old folks' home" at Ortonville, Minnesota, where the Minnesota River begins its flow of four hundred miles to join the Mississippi at St. Paul. Block's haven for old walleyes is the southern extremity of long, narrow Big Stone Lake on the Minnesota-South Dakota border. He operates the Block 'n Tackle Shop at Ortonville and does most of his fishing in the fall, his "off season," the time when walleyes pack into the outlet area to feed on silver bass.

Gearhart Block's skill and persistence, coupled with his proximity to a unique walleye situation, have made him famous as a producer of big walleyes. Having caught as many as seventy-five walleyes over ten pounds in a single season, Block could very well be his country's big-walleye champion.

How long have you been at Big Stone Lake?

I was born here in 1905, and I started to fish when I was about eight years old. That's a mighty long time!

What kind of a lake is Big Stone Lake?

Big Stone Lake is big, thirty-five miles long and not much wider than a mile. It runs about sixteen feet deep in what we call the channel, the deepest part of the lake running right down the middle of its length.

Most of the winter fishing is done in the channel pretty much the length of the lake, although anglers concentrate near access points. The first access going north from Ortonville is at three and a half miles. The second access, where the walleyes come in so strong in the fall, is seven miles up the lake from here, near the rearing pond. You can fish the walleyes in the shallows in the fall of the year, sometimes well into December. But you can catch walleyes the length of the lake, for that matter.

Where do you fish for the big walleyes?

We get the big ones down here by the Ottertail Outlet at the start of the Minnesota River. They come in there around the fifteenth of September and it improves from then on. In 1970 it was over on November 21. In 1971 they didn't start 'til November 22, and we made our biggest hits around December 15. In fact, I was standing there with a hundred dollar bill willing to bet with anyone that we wouldn't see a walleye under ten pounds for three nights. And we didn't, either!

Then it's open water fishing for your big ones?

It's open water fishing, even when much of the lake is frozen. There's always an acre or so of open water near the outlet. It's a matter of casting from shore — all artificials. We use big plugs called Hell-Cats, made by the Whopper Stopper bait company in Sherman, Texas. They look something like big Rapalas and Rebels and come in different sizes and patterns. I doctor them up with a home-made paint job. They run deep, right along the bottom. I use a long heavy-duty spinning outfit to heave those big plugs out there. A strong south wind helps me with distance. We get out there into seven or eight feet of water.

It's all-night fishing, between sundown and sunup. One big secret, a real must for those shallow water walleyes, is whisper silence. After all, we're casting into shallow water! Any footsteps or racket can be sensed by those fish. You can't mess around and be noisy when you're fishin' for walleyes.

How frequent are those big fish? There must be lots of fishermen there when the big ones move in.

Yes. There are lots of fishermen. When the big ones were in this fall we got, oh, ten or twelve a night. When smaller ones came in we got as high as thirty-eight, mixed sizes.

Do you fish especially for big walleyes when you go down to the outlet?

Oh, yes! I want big walleyes. If I get small ones I turn 'em loose. I want lunkers, over ten pounds. Unless I want a couple for eating I turn loose anything under ten pounds. I have my pliers with me and, if necessary, I'll cut the treble hook so I don't injure the fish. The thing to do is to have extra hooks along.

  And you can't have a lot of light for my kind of fishing. A guy'll drive down there and put his car lights on me and he'll kill me deader than a mackerel.

What's the best catch you've ever made?

The best I made down at the outlet was twenty-two walleyes in one evening. That included six mighty big ones, I'll tell you. But I've also gone maybe twenty-two days without a strike. So it isn't all sunshine.

How has your fishing changed over the years?

I think years ago we caught more walleyes. It seemed we got all the fish we wanted every time we went out. Now, this lake is coming back. Big Stone is a good walleye lake. In fact, we're getting more real big ones than we did years ago. When I was a kid we used spoon hooks. But we used frogs, chubs, you name it. That spoon hook used to be a great walleye bait. We used to row slowly and drag that spoon hook on a cane pole and catch all kinds of walleyes. No leaders then — tied it right on some old heavy line.

Do you use a leader now, when you're casting for big ones?

No. No leader and no swivel. But I do use a snap for changing baits. Swivels are out. With swivels you lose half of the action of the lure, regardless of their merits otherwise. That's my idea, anyway. A lot of guys will go out there and want to use a great big heavy leader and put their lead a foot and a half ahead of the lure. I use no leader, and I put my sinker, maybe a quarter-ounce or a little more, about eight inches ahead of my big lure. That outfit hugs the bottom pretty close.

  Now, one time there were about seventy guys down there

fishing. There were four walleyes caught, and I caught all four of 'em. All over ten pounds! One guy standing there said, "Well, he's lucky."

The guy next to him said, "No, I won't buy a line like that. He's more than lucky. That bait was riding where it belonged and doin' the right thing!"

Do you ever use jigs, Gearhart?

I don't. But some fellows use yellow and white doll flies. A friend of mine jigs at the outlet during our fall run, but he doesn't get the big ones. He gets a lot of fish, though.

Is most of the lake bottom clean?

No. No. No. She's weedy, quite weedy. Algae is a major problem in the summer. A lot of farming country is drained by water flowing into this lake. 1971 was actually good as far as the algae was concerned.

Are you ever heckled by skeptics?

You bet. I've been insulted more than once. I had one guy imply that we were a bunch of liars here. I told him if he wanted to put his money where his mouth was, he could come on up and fish with us — we had *our* money ready. But he was just a talker. Them kind of guys are worth a dime a dozen. Talkers. He probably never caught a big walleye and doesn't know the first thing about it.

Do those walleyes that jam into the outlet area have free travelling down the river?

The walleyes can go from Big Stone Lake into the river. Most of those we get appear to be lake walleyes. I guess it's been since the early sixties that we've had access to so many big ones.

What do the fishermen get who angle out in the lake as the season goes on?

Well, they get plenty of fish, when they bite. They get more regular-sized walleyes, not so many big ones. Once in a while they'll get a big one, but the catches are mixed. I've seen 'em bring in ten-pounders and eleven-pounders right in the summertime.

Up north of here a few miles we've got four islands right in the channel, called Manhattan Reef. And, boy, there's a lot of walleyes up in there.

In the winter they put fish houses in the channel areas of the lake, anywhere from eight to sixteen feet of water. They jig out walleyes on Pimples, Pflueger's Limpers, and Doo-Jiggers.

What makes those big walleyes cram into the outlet area in the fall?

The fish are attracted to that area. The Ottertail Power Co. outlet throws warm water out into the lake in the area where the Minnesota River begins. That warmer water pours in at a rate of probably thousands of gallons a minute. That keeps the lake open, and it attracts silver bass, especially in the fall. That's what the big walleyes feed on, those silver bass, hardly anything else. Occasionally a bullhead shows up in a walleye stomach, and once in a while there'll be a little minnow in there. Where the feed packs in, in that outlet area, the walleyes are close by.

Don't the minnow fishermen catch fish there?

It's funny. During that fall run they won't hit minnows. In the spring up the lake they go wild over minnows. Throughout most of the season they use suckers and fatheads. Shiners are okay in the spring. We get 'em right out of the lake, and the creeks are full of shiners, too.

It seems they get bigger fish on the bigger minnows. One year I remember we had to use sucker minnows about six inches long. If you went four inches, or seven inches, it just wouldn't do it. Of course when the ice fishermen use Swedish Pimples or those other winter spoons, they hook a fathead in the mouth. They kind of forget about the big minnows then.

What happens during the winter months at your outlet area where you get the big ones in fall? Do anglers congregate there at night during those times?

No. She plays out in early December, often before that. Those walleyes gotta cross cold water in the shallows before they get there. It's shallow and the water's too cold for 'em. That's what seems to be the case. I've been down there around Christmas. Once I got a fifteen-pound northern and a twelve-pounder. But I've seen darn few walleyes caught there in winter.

You've landed a fifteen-pound walleye. Do you recall that trip?

I fished one night and got two walleyes. At about two-thirty I lost a big one. I fished out the rest of that night with no more fish and missed the few hits I had. Then the wind turned into the south, blowing out away from our shore, adding quite a bit to your casting distance. She was blowin' pretty good, so you could really get your bait out there.

Well, that day, the day after I caught the two, I hollered for my wife to get an early supper. I wanted to go fishing. She told me, "You're loony. You're crazy with that fishing."

I said, "I'll bet those walleyes are in there."

So I went down, and do you know that on the first cast, my very first one, I hit that fifteen-pounder, and caught eleven more walleyes after that. Of course, I had to return

Gearhart Block with a 15-pounder, two 10-pounders, an 8-pounder, and two in the 5-pound class.

six of them to stay at my limit. Those fish were really in there. Another guy came down and he got a nine-pounder. That was about eight o'clock — I had been fishing for about two hours. Another guy got an eleven-pounder. Then they got one little walleye and two northerns the rest of the night.

You see, I had a real break that night. There wasn't one man come down there 'til these guys pulled in about eight o'clock, when I already had plenty of fish. There was no noise. When they come down there and stumble over things and kick rocks around, or drag a landing net on the rocks, then there goes the night's fishing. Right there.

You use really big spinning rods. What's the object of that?

Oh, casting distance, big fish. And I like the big guides for freezing temperatures. They don't freeze up so fast. I can still wind in with a little ice on the guides.

Do you use night crawlers at all?

Well, I fish during that big fish run in the fall, and that's about it. Otherwise I'm too busy in my tackle shop. So I use those artificials and that's all. But night crawlers are getting to be quite the bait in the summertime around here. They put crawlers on spinners and harnesses. Those harnesses are good rigs in the summer and they get a lot of fish. They use Flatfish and other plugs and load 'em with worms. This worm fishing is mostly trolling, of course.

I haven't trolled for ten years, myself. I don't get to fish in the summertime, and I don't get to fish all winter 'til March. That's for crappies. But the walleye fishermen push fish houses onto Big Stone Lake in big numbers once the ice is a foot thick or so. They cram in there by the hundreds. If there's enough ice and not too much snow, there'll be between one and two thousand fish houses by that first Highway 7 public access, up by the islands.

When you cast for those big walleyes, how do you retrieve the lure?

Just a steady pull. A slow retrieve. I wind her in slowly — no pumping or nothin'! I just reel. I've seen these guys pumpin' and jiggin', and what not, with those lures. But you can outfish them three and four to one with a steady retrieve. I'm not saying a pump is no good altogether. It just hasn't worked for me. With jigs it's different. You've got to give them action.

Some respectable fishermen talk about the "secrets" of walleye fishing. Do you have secrets?

Every angler who puts in the hours has secrets and tricks up his sleeve. I'd like to believe I have some, little things that make a difference, things you kind of keep to yourself. You'll see a guy like Heine go down there with Doll Flies and catch walleyes when I couldn't and maybe the next guy couldn't on those jigs. Same way with those Pimples in winter. We can sit alongside a good Pimple guy and he might get five or ten or more walleyes to our one. What are we doin' wrong, we ask. But more likely he's just doin' somethin' different.

JIGGING FOR RIVER WALLEYES
An Interview with Bob McGarry

Bob McGarry divides his time between walleye fishing and selling insurance in Stillwater, Minnesota. His fishing takes place on the picturesque St. Croix River which flows from northwestern Wisconsin in a southerly direction for 164 miles to its juncture with the Mississippi near Hastings, south of the Twin Cities. Bob has a keen understanding of river walleyes and is a master of the jigging technique.

Bob, what kind of bottom structure do you look for when fishing the river?

Well, the St. Croix River between Stillwater and Taylors Falls is composed of a number of islands and points. My favorite type of walleye fishing is to hit the various points between here and the northern part of the river, some distance from shore. As the current comes down, it'll break on both sides of these points, and this is where the walleyes hang out in early morning, around sunup, for feeding purposes. I like to anchor and jig off these points, as well as some points jutting out from shore.

Where do you anchor in relation to a point?

I go upstream a little bit, either east or west of a point. You see, the river runs north and south here. It's interesting, because sometimes the walleyes will be on the east side of the point, sometimes on the west. This is independent of wind and other weather factors. I simply have to investigate this on every fishing trip.

Is rock or gravel bottom associated with these points?

Actually, it's primarily sand. The current from Stillwater on up is rather fast. As it hits Stillwater it widens into Lake St. Croix and slows down, and the bottom is softer. But between Stillwater and Taylors Falls the current is fast and the bottom is sandy in most places, although some backwaters have muck bottom. For example, up at Wolf Bay near Wolf's Marina there are logging chips from back in the old days on the bottom, and that area is generally poor for walleyes, although shore fishermen do catch fish near a creek mouth there in the spring. But that isn't my cup of tea.

How do they fish when they cast out from shore?

They cast with jig-minnow combinations. That's about all they use, even the old-timers. There is a favorite spot right off the fill on the Wisconsin side of the bridge here. Fellows have fished that for years. It's a good evening spot. They seem to come in there best at night. I don't know whether it's the light from the bridge that attracts 'em or what, but they move in there at night and they've taken some nice-sized fish there. That spot is good from the Opening until, oh, maybe the first of July. But that spot has tapered off some since the power plant's operation began.

You say you jig from an anchored boat. What about trolling?

Any number of people have success trolling on the river, using the Rapala, Lazy Ike, or that sort of thing.

Do these trollers watch for bottom structure? Or do they troll randomly across the river?

No, most of them know what they're doing. They fish structure. In fact they troll back and forth in the areas where I'm anchored. Again, it's off these points or in holes where it's rocky and so forth.

For the most part, is your fishing in shallow water?

I've caught walleyes in the early morning when they're feeding off these points, specifically in the early season when the water's still cool — in water as shallow as one foot! Of course the water is murky, remember, and it drops off right near there. She drops into about five feet near shore in the spring, then falls off from there. Even the channel itself isn't much more than twelve to fourteen feet at normal river levels. But as you go down river into the lake she gets much deeper. Down there the fishing gets better in summer while it falls off up here.

Then the better walleye fishing shifts downstream into the lake as the season progresses?

It's fair to say that, yes. Every year we're getting more boat traffic in the northern stretches above Stillwater, where I fish in the spring and fall. The channel is narrow and the boats throw quite a wake. There's no question about it, the boaters disturb fishing here. So you have to go down river as the summer progresses, partially because of this boat traffic, and also because of the increased water temperatures. This probably drives the walleyes into the deeper holes down there. There are deep holes and rocky reefs out in the lake itself not betrayed by islands. You have to know where they are. They use sonar or sounding lines for locating the spots.

Another factor seems to be the power plant up here. Before that was operating we used to catch more in quantity and quality above the St. Croix bridge at Stillwater than we do now. We still catch fish north, that's for sure, but other river veterans will tell you what I've said, that the plant has affected fishing up here. We have a hole about a mile from here that was just terrific for walleyes. I don't know if it's a thermal barrier caused by the plant or what, but since its operation started we just haven't enjoyed the size and the consistency that we used to have, although the fellows down below here have been doing all right in the summer.

Where do these river walleyes spawn?

Down on the Mississippi below where the St. Croix joins it, there are dams, and walleyes spawn in the stretches below the dams. On the St. Croix, a lot of walleyes head for the shallower stretches north of here toward Osceola and Taylors Falls. The river is shallow and very narrow up there, and sandy with deposits of rock and gravel.

How does water level affect your fishing?

That's an interesting thing. I'm sure if you talked to five different fishermen you'd get that many ideas. For my part,

Bob McGarry fishes the picturesque St. Croix River.

I've had better fishing when the waters push a foot and a half to two feet above normal. No more than that. We've had floods here, as you probably know, and in those years the fishing was simply no good at all until after the water went down. And then sometimes heavy rain would raise it way back up again. So some of those years were practically written off. I like it best when we have a normal spring. I have my best success with water levels just slightly above normal — I can't really say why. But that's what experience has shown.

Do you stop fishing during the summer months when fishing slacks up here?

I do taper it off, yes, but I pick it up again in the fall. The fishing picks up then, though it isn't like it is in the spring. I use the same jigging methods in the fall, but I prefer darker colors then.

What kind of minnows do you use on the jig, if you do use them?

The fathead minnow seems to be the best, but they're hard to get here. One time we trapped some on our own in a lake west of town, and we never had such success with minnows. They were black males, real dark, and the wall-eyes wanted those minnows like they were T-bone steaks! Of course, those minnows were fresh. Some of the store-bought ones just aren't any good. And to me, if you have a bad batch of minnows you're wasting your time.

What's the maximum depth you toss the jig into?

I would say that my maximum is ten to twelve feet. Beyond that depth you lose the effectiveness of your jig on the river. The shallower the water, the more effective the jig becomes. You see, on the river it's more difficult than on the lake, especially in early spring when you have a fairly fast current, because you throw the jig out and all it does is float. Normally, you wait 'til the current carries it downstream to the end of the line you cast out, then begin the retrieve. Until then you'd get no action, even if you jig the rod.

Do you have any jig favorites?

There's a fellow in town who makes the ones I like. I've tried others and I have to believe that his are the best, at least for fishing here. He makes them in different weights and colors, of course. They're good jigs, bucktails. Sometimes he makes them plain, just the lead head, with no paint, and the tail. One year he had some that were a dull green and you couldn't get enough of those. I would say that in darker water and darker times of day the dark colors are most effective. If I'm out there early in the morning before sunrise — it's not real dark because I'm not an avid nighttime fisherman — I'll use fairly dark colors. After the sun comes up I'll change to a brighter color, and that seems to work.

What size jig do you prefer?

It depends on current. Quarter-ounce is my favorite. Three-eighths is about the heaviest I go and only in deep water and fast current. The smaller eighth-ounce jig is really too light for the river. She won't go down — just lays out there without settling to the bottom.

How about retrieve? Do you give the jig a good pumping action or more of a straight wind-in?

Well, when you toss it out and it gets downstream, give it a fast jigging action to start with. Then slow down, because current fishing with a jig is different from a lake. The smallest tug on that jig will give it lots of action against the current. The jig is definitely being jigged, though, and is hopping up and down all the time.

Lake fishermen are very weather-conscious. Is the river fisherman as concerned about wind, rain, clouds, and other elements?

We certainly don't have the rough water and safety elements to worry about. And I don't believe our fishing is as closely geared to weather factors as are lake situations. Your frontal systems and changes in pressure affect our fishing. But other than that, well, wind affects it some. For me, here, a southeast wind is not good. A north wind or any northerly combination seems to be the best. Rain doesn't bother it, and I've been out in snowstorms when we've had really good fishing.

How do these walleyes run for size?

The last couple years they've been smaller, but still running about two pounds, nice fish. But I will say this, knowing that fishermen tend to brag a little — three years ago and before that, in the spring, we were averaging five and six pounds! And we'd catch numbers of these fish, too. I could go out before work and be back before nine in the morning with a limit of five-pound and six-pound walleyes. It was unbelievable, and this would go on day after day for quite a while. My biggest is nine pounds, maybe a little better — nothing spectacular, but nice.

Getting back to tackle, how heavy a line test do you recommend for walleye jigs?

I go heavy compared to most jiggers. I stick with ten-pound test line. Of course the better stuff has a smaller diameter, so it's just as effective as the ordinary six. I used to use an eight-pound line, but I switched because of one incident.

You see, every spring Stillwater has a "Sports Day" when we have professional athletes up here for some fishing. Two years ago I had two pros out with me and I lost the biggest fish I ever had on. And I don't think ten-pound line would have frightened him out of biting. So I went to the ten-pound stuff.

I tie the jig right on the line, using no snaps or swivel-snaps.

Are rods and reels important? What do you use?

I guess you'd classify my rods as medium-action, not really light weight tackle. I stick with a couple poles I like, a seven-footer and a shorter one. The rod selection depends on when I'm fishing, the height of the water, the current, and so forth. The reels are push-button spin-cast models.

You know, it's a funny thing. If you've got the right bait, and you know what you're doing, you could fish with almost anything. That's my theory anyway. So many people make a fuss over rod and reel choice when it's really the terminal tackle that counts. At least that's the way it is with walleyes. If you don't know how to use your gear, when to fish, and where to fish, the rod and reel don't make much difference.

Are you troubled with snags in the river?

Yes, snags there are! You bet. Not rocks so much, but sunken logs and other debris. We get a lot of wash in the spring with high water, and these logs come down from up-stream. I always carry extra jigs.

What about fish other than walleyes?

Smallmouth and rock bass hit our jigs. So do saugers and northerns. And there are lots of silver bass. Walleyes might feed on the young of these fish. I really haven't studied their diets.

Can you recall some of the best fishing you've had on the St. Croix?

Three years ago we used to own a houseboat. We'd go out at night and anchor and sleep out there. In the morning, first thing, we'd go fishing. This one particular morning it was snowing. This was after the season opened in spring. It was cold and the wind was from the northeast. There were three of us fishing, and every time we cast — this is no exaggeration — there was either a bite or a fish. In our limit of eighteen walleyes there wasn't a one under five pounds. We got those fish at one of my favorite spots just north of town.

Of all the fish in the river, why do you favor walleyes?

There are always exceptions, and always the unexpected — that's what makes walleye fishing interesting. I recall one time when I had the family out on the houseboat. We were on our way back to town at about five o'clock on a hot summer afternoon. Boats were going up and down the river, making all kinds of noise and racket. Inside the channel I told the boy, "Let's anchor here."

We cast out and caught eight walleyes. It was still midday according to daylight saving time. Ordinarily if I had told some guy, "Let's go fishing," at five o'clock on a hot summer afternoon, he'd say I was crazy. Those fish don't follow a standard pattern all the time. Walleyes are hard to figure out.

CONCLUSION

It was about five-thirty in the afternoon on a hot fifth of July. The lake was quiet and the sun was still high, with at least several hours of daylight remaining. I decided to go fishing. In a half-hour I had everything ready. The outboards were gassed, the minnows aboard, as were tackle, marker jug, landing net, rods, and stringer.

I headed for what we call the Matton Flat, a large mud flat out in Mille Lacs about three miles from my home. Well, I trolled along the east side of that flat, sometimes on top, sometimes in the deep, but mostly along the drop-off where I thought I belonged. I fished for more than an hour without a walleye bite and was tempted to quit.

Yet the lake was nice and I had a depth finder with me — a new plaything at that time. So I thought I'd give them another chance by running out a mile or so to the other end of the flat. On the way I watched the depth finder dial and was irritated by the oars rattling on the seats. I had second thoughts about staying on the lake any longer. But I kept going.

The depth reading was a steady twenty-three feet for about five minutes, then she tumbled down to thirty in a second. I slowed the boat and circled back, throwing out my white Hi-lex jug marker as soon as I was back up on top. I baited up again with the expectation that goes along with throwing a line in fresh, although I admit my optimism was limited.

I trolled the edge for no more than twenty yards beyond the marker when I hooked a nice walleye, about two pounds, which renewed my enthusiasm a little. I turned the boat and let my line out again, holding that edge faithfully. Before I covered the short distance back to the marker I had another fish. And that's how it went for the next hour and a half. Those walleyes were bunched up in there and biting like mad. I caught more than twenty good walleyes, saving a limit of six three-pounders.

The sun was still an hour from setting when I left that hot spot for home, still numbed from my unexpected success. On the ride back I didn't hear the oars rattle. The boat plowed along faithfully, and the engines were running more smoothly than usual, I thought. It was a good trip. Nice fish. I knew where to go in the morning.

If I may echo Bob McGarry, walleyes are my cup of tea!

Author Joe Fellegy, Jr.

NORTH AMERICAN WALLEYE DISTRIBUTION GUIDE

The following list of walleye waters was drawn from state and provincial fishing guide booklets and correspondence with fisheries supervisors. As this book has emphasized, any list of walleye "hot spots" is necessarily incomplete because of the walleye's wide distribution in certain areas and because of the unpredictable nature of walleye fishing. Also, in recent years walleyes have been successfully introduced well outside their natural range, creating new fisheries and new sport.

Alabama

Walleyes are present in several of Alabama's major river systems, even as far south as Mobile. Walleyes are found in the following rivers: Tennessee, Tombigee, Alabama, Cahaba, Tensaw, Lower Tallapoosa, and parts of the Coosa River system. Walleyes are abundant enough to provide a fishery in the Tennessee, Cahaba, and the Lower Tallapoosa rivers. State record: 8 pounds, 4 ounces, caught in the Tallapoosa near Wetumpka, Alabama, on May 17, 1970. There are unconfirmed reports of walleyes weighing 11 pounds.

Arizona

Arizona hosts substantial walleye populations in several lakes. Walleyes here have exhibited fantastic growth rates, with sac-fry reaching three pounds in two years. Walleyes occur in Apache, Canyon, and Saguaro lakes on the Salt River chain of lakes, and in Lake Powell on the Colorado River.

Arkansas

Bull Shoals, Norfolk, and Greers Ferry lakes have the best populations of Arkansas walleyes. Beaver, Ouachita, De-Gray, Greeson, Catherine, and Ozark lakes also yield walleyes. Rivers where walleyes are found include Eleven Point, Spring, White, Little Red, Ouachita, Saline, and Caddo. Walleyes are native to most of the cooler rivers in Arkansas and maintain their numbers by natural reproduction. Stocking is confined to lakes. State record: 19 pounds, 3 ounces.

California

Walleyes from the Missisquoi River, Vermont, were introduced in the Sacramento River in 1874 with no apparent survival. Experimental annual plants starting in 1959 established small populations of walleyes in Casitas, Cachuma, Puddingstone, and El Capitan reservoirs. However, no natural reproduction has been observed.

Colorado

Walleyes were successfully introduced in Colorado in 1949 and have become an important game fish in that state. The following waters yield walleyes: Horsetooth Reservoir, west of Fort Collins; Adobe Creek Reservoir (Blue Lakes), north of Las Animas; Bonny Reservoir, south of Idalia; Cherry Creek Reservoir, south of Denver; Boyd Reservoir, east of Loveland, in Loveland; Queens Reservoir, north of Lamar; Jumbo Reservoir, south of Sedgwick; Jackson Lake, west of Orchard; Loveland Lake, in Loveland; Sterling Reservoir, northwest of Sterling; Two Buttes Reservoir, north of Lamar. State record: approximately 13 pounds.

Connecticut

An occasional walleye shows up in Lakes Lillinonah and Zoar, but no worthwhile fishing exists. Despite stocking in many Connecticut lakes, walleyes failed to become established.

Georgia

The best walleye waters in Georgia are Lakes Blueridge,

Burton, Hartwell, and Chatuge. Walleyes are also found in Lake Lanier and in Lake Allatoona, although these are not considered "fishable" at present. Walleye populations in Georgia were established by fingerling stocking, then maintained by natural reproduction.

Idaho

An occasional walleye shows up in Pend Oreille Lake, apparently "drifts" from the Clark Fork River in Montana.

Illinois

Despite a limited walleye distribution in Illinois, dependable walleye fishing exists in the Fox Chain o' Lakes and in the following rivers where walleyes occur naturally: Rock, Kankakee, and northern portions of the Mississippi, Ohio, and Wabash. State record: 14 pounds, from Kankakee River, 1961.

Indiana

The better walleye spots include Kankakee River in northwest Indiana; Quick Creek Reservoir, Scott County; Salamonie Reservoir, Huntington County; and Cataract Lake, Owen-Putnam County.

Iowa

Many Iowa waters provide quality walleye fishing, such as the Des Moines and Racoon rivers. Clear, Spirit, West Okoboji, and East Okoboji are very productive natural walleye lakes in northwestern Iowa. The state operates an extensive hatchery and stocking program, producing about 100 million walleye fry annually.

Kansas

Walleyes were stocked in the large federal reservoirs in about 1950 and succeeding years. Walleyes are now doing well in most of these Corps of Engineers and Bureau of

Reclamation reservoirs, which range in size from about sixteen thousand to twenty-two thousand acres. In most of these lakes natural reproduction maintains satisfactory walleye populations. Kansas has a hatchery and stocking program for new lakes and for those in need of stocking. Some of the better walleye reservoirs are Kirwin, Wilson, Norton, Kanapolis, Milford, Tuttle Creek, Cheney, and Pomona.

Kentucky

Walleyes are present in Lake Cumberland and its tributaries, and also in the Cumberland River below the dam. A number of years ago Lake Cumberland hosted a population of large walleyes, usually over thirteen pounds when caught. They are also found in the Licking, Green, Kentucky, and Ohio rivers, although not in large numbers. Walleyes were stocked in Barren and Rough River lakes with moderate success.

Maryland

Walleyes, called "yellow pikeperch" and "Susquehanna Salmon" in Maryland, are found in the large Maryland reservoirs and in the Susquehanna River. State record: 8 pounds, 12 ounces.

Massachusetts

The Connecticut River in the vicinity of Turners Falls in northwestern Massachusetts produces walleyes in an otherwise "non-walleye" state.

Michigan

Walleyes inhabit many lakes and streams throughout Michigan and surrounding Great Lakes waters. A list of good spots might include the following: Lake Gogebic, Gogebic and Ontonagon Counties; Munuscong Lake, Chippewa County; Manistique Lake, Mackinac and Luce Counties; Burt Lake, Cheboygan County; Cadillac and Mitchell lakes,

A chunky walleye from a lake on the Kansas prairie, taken on a minnow and Prescott pike hook no. 2.

Wexford County; Hodenpyle Backwaters, Wexford County; Huron River Chain, southern Livingston County; Muskegon River and Lake, Muskegon and Newaygo Counties; Indian Lake, Schoolcraft County; Big Rapids Pond, Moreley Pond, and Rogers Pond, Mecosta County; Little Bay de Noc, Delta County; Big Creek Impoundment, Crawford County.

Minnesota

In Minnesota the walleye is the "state fish." Minnesota's Department of Natural Resources operates the world's largest hatchery and stocking program for walleyes. Minnesota has more natural walleye water than any other state. (See pp. 6-9 and pp. 109-116.)

Mississippi

The walleye is widely distributed in the Tombigbee River system, although not abundant. Walleye waters include the Tombigbee River, Buttahatchie River and Slipsey Creek, Luxapalila Creek and Yellow Creek, Noxubee River and Hashuqua Creek, Sucarnoochee Creek and Ponta Creek, Mackey's Creek, Brown's reek, Bull Mountain Creek, Weaver's Creek, and McCower's Creek.

Missouri

The walleye is probably most abundant in the Mississippi River above the mouth of the Missouri, in Current River, and in the Osage River above Lake of the Ozarks. Walleyes are present in most of the large reservoirs.

Montana

The two most popular walleye spots are Nelson Reservoir, a large private irrigation company reservoir just north of Malta; and Yellowtail Reservoir, a large Bureau of Reclamation reservoir on the Bighorn River south of Hardin. The westernmost places where walleyes appear in fair numbers

Minnesota

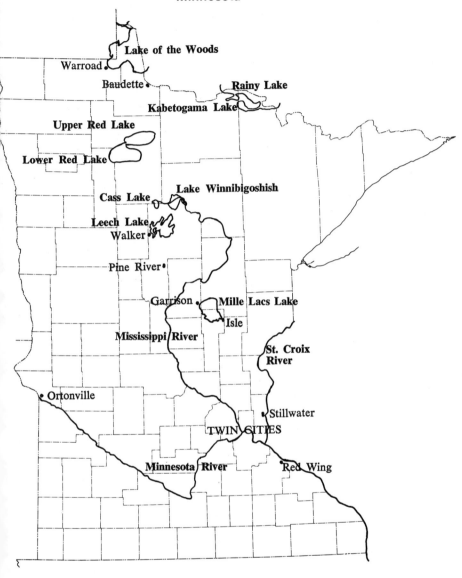

Minnesota offers nine months of walleye fishing starting on the Saturday closest to May 15 and running continuously until February 15. Daily and possession limits are 6 per angler in Minnesota, where there is no minimum walleye size.

are Holter and Hauser reservoirs on the Missouri River just east of Helena. The latter are primarily trout waters where live bait is illegal.

Nevada

Since 1969, walleye fingerlings have been stocked annually in Rye Patch Reservoir on the Humboldt River in Pershing County. The fish exhibited an excellent growth rate weighing two pounds and over by the middle of 1972. The first legal walleye season in Nevada was scheduled for 1973 with the fishing outlook good in Rye Patch and in the river below it.

New Hampshire

As pollution abatement increases, so should the walleye fishing. Good fisheries exist in the Merrimack River downstream from Hooksett, and in the Connecticut River downstream from Moore Reservoir.

New Jersey

The section of the Delaware River that is upstream from Belvidere provides noteworthy walleye angling. According to fisheries officials, that fishery is respectable and "underutilized." There is no closed season or size limit on the river.

New Mexico

Walleyes have been in New Mexican waters since 1940. The greatest populations are found in the three largest bodies of warm water in the state: Elephant Butte, Conchas, and Ute. There is a stable population in Alamogordo Reservoir near Fort Sumner and a relatively small population in Caballo Lake near Truth or Consequences, as well as in Lake McMillan south of Artesia. The situation is changing; walleye populations are increasing in "fair" waters, bringing them into the "good" class, and they are also spreading to new waters.

New York

In New York the walleye is often called "pike perch" and "Oneida Lake Pike." Excellent walleye angling occurs in many lakes and streams during both open water and ice fishing seasons. Walleyes are taken from the Chenango, Delaware, Allegany, Chemung, Hudson, Niagara, Mohawk, Seneca, and Susquehanna rivers, to name a few. Champlain, Oneida, Erie, Ontario, Tupper, Sacandaga, Red, and Otisco are among the walleye lakes. State record: 15 pounds, 3 ounces, taken from the Chemung River in 1952 by Blanche Baker.

North Carolina

Walleyes are most numerous in the rivers and lakes of the Tennessee River system in the western part of the state. However, walleyes occur as far east as the Roanoke River and in Lake James of the Atlantic drainage. While several large streams yield walleyes, the best fishing is in the larger reservoirs, the best of which are: Santeetlah in Graham County; Glenville, Jackson County; Hiwassee, Cherokee County; Fontana, Graham and Swain Counties; James, McDowell and Burke Counties. State record: 13 pounds, 4 ounces, taken from Santeetlah in 1966.

North Dakota

Lake Sakakawea (Garrison Reservoir), Oahe Reservoir, and Jamestown Reservoir provide most of North Dakota's walleye action, which is quite good at times. Lake Sakakawea holds world record sauger catches.

Ohio

Lake Erie and various inland waters hold walleyes. In Lake Erie, the Bass Islands and Kelleys Island areas produce walleyes the year round. Summer adds the Port Clinton reefs and the Huron-Vermilion region to the fishing grounds. Generally, walleyes are most abundant in the western third of Lake Erie. Other walleye waters in northern Ohio are Bellevue Reservoir no. 5, Ferguson Reservoir, Findlay Reservoir, Maumee River, Norwalk Reservoir no. 2, Sandusky River, Wauseon Reservoir no. 2, Berlin Reservoir, Grand River, Lake Milton, Mosquito Creek, and Pymatuning Lake. Walleye waters in central and southern Ohio include Dillon Dam, Seneca Reservoir, Big Walnut Creek, Hoover Dam, Indian Lake, and Kiser Lake.

Oklahoma

A walleye stocking program begun in 1962 has introduced walleyes in every major reservoir. Walleye populations are present in a dozen lakes. The two best producers are Canton Lake northwest of Oklahoma City, and Altus Lugert Reservoir north of Altus in southwestern Oklahoma.

Pennsylvania

Walleyes have been stocked in nearly every county in Pennsylvania, mostly in the larger streams and in both large and small lakes. Pymatuning Lake (Crawford County), Lake Wallenpaupack (Pike and Wayne Counties), and Lake Erie are prime waters. A host of other lakes and streams, including the Allegheny, Juniata, and Susquehanna Rivers, yield fine catches. Walleyes up to fifteen pounds have been caught by Pennsylvania anglers.

South Carolina

Fifty-eight-thousand-acre Lake Hartwell on the northwest border with Georgia provides the best walleye fishing. This reservoir was stocked with adult and fry walleye upon its completion in the early 1960s. By 1972 walleyes approaching eight pounds were taken. Walleye and sauger show up in Clark Hill Reservoir, thirty miles downstream from Lake Hartwell. Murray Lake in central South Carolina hosts a growing walleye population.

Late winter ice fishing on Lake Champlain in Vermont produced this nice walleye.

South Dakota

Enemy Swim, Pickerel, Clear, Roy, Poinsett, and Kampeska lakes in eastern South Dakota are among the better walleye lakes. The Missouri River and its reservoir lakes, especially Oahe, Sharpe, and Francis Case, provide fast-growing walleyes. The areas below Oahe, Big Bend, and Fort Randall dams are also good.

Tennessee

Walleyes bite best in April, May, and June, but show up all year. There are no closed seasons or size limits; the daily limit is ten. The best walleye lakes are Center Hill, Dale Hollow, Norris, and Watauga. Lakes with fair walleye populations are Percy Priest, Woods, and Old Hickory (where the world's record, a twenty-five-pound walleye, was taken in 1960). Growth rate is fast here, with fish maturing a year earlier than in the northern U.S.

Texas

Walleyes continue to grow in popularity in Texas. Lake Meredith, in the Panhandle, is the best walleye lake, with "average" fish weighing three to four pounds. Lake Diversion (Wichita Falls area) and San Angelo Reservoir support good walleye populations, as does Lake Cypress Springs in northeastern Texas. State record: 8 pounds, 14 ounces.

Utah

Although walleyes are not native to Utah, they occur in healthy numbers in several Utah lakes. Utah Lake, a remnant of Lake Bonneville, now supports an excellent walleye population. The best fishing occurs during the spawning season, beginning as early as the first or second week of March. Rocky shoreline areas, the Provo River and the Provo boat harbor rate as the most popular spots. Live bait fish are prohibited.

Walleyes and several catfish from the TVA country of Tennessee, where Old Hickory Lake boasts the world record, a 25-pound, 3-foot long walleye.

Willard Bay Reservoir, a dike-separated bay of Great Salt Lake, already holds four-pound and five-pound walleyes and should provide excellent walleye fishing in the future. The same holds true for Lake Powell, formed by the Glen Canyon Dam on the Colorado River near Page, Arizona. When full, Lake Powell will be about 190 miles long with many bays and water-filled canyons. Already it has a fair walleye population, including some large ones.

Walleyes have also been introduced in some less important Utah waters.

Vermont

Vermont boasts open water and ice fishing for walleyes. Walleyes are taken the length of Lake Champlain and from the following waters: Missisquoi River, White River, Connecticut River, Lake Memphremagog, Lamoille River, Otter Creek, Lake Bomoseen, Waterbury Reservoir, and West River.

Virginia

Virginia's best walleye water is the New River, especially below Claytor Dam where fish as large as seventeen pounds (the state record) have been taken in late fall and winter. Walleyes also do well in Claytor Lake. Anglers also take walleyes in Clinch River and from the Roanoke River system, most notably in the Pigg River arm of Leesville Lake. Kerr Reservoir yields walleyes. The Game Commission has stocked walleyes in Lakes Gaston, Chesdin, Buggs Island, Leesville, and Smith Mountain.

Washington

Few Washington waters supply the correct habitat for walleyes. However, walleyes have been taken from Banks Lake, in the stretch of the Columbia below the Grand Coulee Dam, in the Spokane River, and in Long Lake near Spokane.

Conservation officer Jerry Dahlberg with walleye fishermen at the
Provo Boat Harbor on Utah Lake, Utah.

West Virginia

The major self-sustaining walleye population in West Virginia occurs in Summersville Reservoir east of Charleston. During the early 1970s, stocking led to the development of a good fishery at Sutton Reservoir. Walleye fry will be stocked in all new impoundments where water quality and habitat are adequate. Major catches of river walleyes occur in the Elk and Greenbrier rivers, and also in the New River below Bluestone Dam.

Wisconsin

Wisconsin is a top walleye state, with walleyes taken from most lakes and streams of any size. The larger lakes are usually the best walleye lakes. Most famous has been Lake Winnebago and adjoining rivers. A seventy-seven-page guide entitled "Wisconsin Walleye Waters" is available from the Department of Natural Resources, Box 450, Madison, Wisconsin 53701.

Wyoming

Three prominent lakes have substantial walleye fishing: Boysen Reservoir in Fremont County, Keyhole Reservoir in Crook County, and Seminoe Reservoir in Carbon County.

Alberta

Alberta's many walleye lakes include the following: Fawcett, Sturgeon, Smoke, Wolf, Moose, Helena, Elinor, Seibert, Ironwood, Touchwood, Baptiste, and Buck. Along with these better known lakes, the lower regions of the large rivers also yield excellent walleye catches. These rivers incude the Athabasca, Peace, Pembina, Beaver, Red Deer, and South Saskatchewan.

British Columbia

While walleyes are less than abundant in British Columbia,

Summersville Reservoir complex in West Virginia, one of the many man-made lakes that have expanded the walleye's range in the United States.

they can be caught. Walleye waters include the Peace, Kiskatinaw, and Beatton rivers (Peace-Mackenzie system); Muskwa River, Fort Nelson River, and Klua lakes (Liard-Mackenzie system).

Manitoba

Manitoba affords excellent walleye fishing in almost all areas of the province, which contains around 100 thousand lakes. Some of the outstanding spots: Grand Rapids, Grass River area, Fairford and Dauphin rivers, White Shell area, Lake Manitoba Narrows, and the Assinboine River. In 1971 there were 191 walleye entries in the Master Angler Awards contest, which requires a minimum weight of eight pounds.

Northwest Territories

Walleyes are abundant in Kasia Lake and Lac St. Theres, and provide good angling in numerous lakes and rivers around Great Slave Lake. Fishing is often best during the spring spawning runs. There is no closed season in the Northwest Territories.

Ontario

Walleyes are caught throughout Ontario, where some of the finest walleye fishing in the world is found — in more lakes and rivers than one could list here. Check with local Chambers of Commerce, the Fisheries Section of the Department of Lands and Forests (Toronto), resorts, and guides for specific information. The Lake of the Woods area of southern Ontario, Lac des Mille Lacs, Minnesota border waters, and the Nipigon region are easily approached from the south.

Quebec

Walleyes are abundant in thousands of lakes and streams in western and central Quebec, but are scarce and sometimes absent in eastern Quebec, particularly on the Gaspé

Fishing for walleyes at Lac-des-Loup in La Verendrye Park in
western Quebec.

Peninsula and in the region north of the Gulf of St. Lawrence. Where walleyes occur fishing can be excellent. A guide to the distribution and abundance of Quebec fish species combined with a map of principal hydrographic basins and other fishing material can be obtained from the Quebec government, Ministry of Tourism, Fishing and Hunting Division, Quebec, Canada.

Saskatchewan

The walleye is the number one game fish here. Walleyes are abundant throughout the province from the southern border to Lake Athabasca in the north. The following watersheds are well-known for excellent walleye populations: Qu' Appelle River system, Saskatchewan River system, and the Churchill River system. Saskatchewan record: 13 pounds, 9 ounces, taken from the Saskatchewan River in 1953.

Yukon Territory

There are reports of walleyes in Gusty Lakes in the southeast corner of the Yukon (60° 30′ long. and 126° 30′ lat. NE) and in the Liard River drainage which flows into the Mackenzie system, although fishable numbers require some searching.

WALLEYE RECIPES

WALLEYE FILLETS AMANDINE

¼ pound butter
Walleye fillets
Salt and pepper
½ cup white wine
Almond slivers, toasted

Place butter in shallow baking pan (select a pan large enough to accommodate fillets without any overlapping). Melt butter in oven until deep golden brown. Season fillets with salt and pepper to taste, dip both sides in butter, and arrange in pan. Boil wine until it is reduced to ¼ cup, then pour over fillets. Bake fillets in a medium oven (350 degrees) or broil, basting once, until fillets flake at the touch of a fork. Just before serving, sprinkle fillets with toasted almond slivers.

(Florence Fritsche, New Ulm, Minnesota)

BAKED WALLEYE IN MUSHROOM SAUCE

Large walleye fillets
¼ cup milk
1 can cream of mushroom soup
1 small can mushroom pieces
¼ teaspoon each salt, pepper, and onion or garlic salt
Wine, if desired
Worcestershire sauce, if desired
2 tablespoons butter
1 tablespoon parsley flakes

Arrange fillets in baking dish. Combine milk, cream of mushroom soup, mushroom pieces, seasonings, and wine or Worcestershire sauce if desired. Pour sauce over fish. Dab with butter and sprinkle with parsley flakes. Bake in 350-degree oven for approximately 25 minutes.

(Edith Barneveld, Wealthwood, Minnesota)

BAKED WALLEYE FILLETS

¼ pound butter or margarine
Walleye fillets (they should be fairly large and thick)
Salt and pepper
Lemon juice
Fresh bread, cut in cubes
Paprika

Melt butter. Dip fillets in butter, then arrange in bottom of pan. Sprinkle salt, pepper, and lemon juice to taste over fish. Cover fillets with bread cubes and sprinkle with paprika. Bake in a 350-degree oven ½ hour, or until bread cubes are well toasted.

(Florence Fritsche, New Ulm, Minnesota)

PAN-FRIED WALLEYE FILLETS

Walleye fillets (if large, cut into pieces)
½ cup milk
1 egg
Cracker, bread, or corn flake crumbs, or cornmeal
Salt, pepper, or other seasonings
Butter (shortening, oil, or bacon drippings may be substituted)

Combine milk and egg by beating lightly with a fork. (More milk and eggs may be needed, depending on quantity of fish.) Dip fillet in egg-milk mixture, then in crumbs, making sure fish is coated completely. Heat butter (at least ¼ inch deep) in frying pan, until hot. Brown both sides of fillets in butter, turning only once. Fillet is done when flesh is white and tender. Serve with tartar sauce, catsup, and lemon wedges.

If fillets are cooked over a hot outdoor fire, try dipping them in pancake batter and frying them in cooking oil, which withstands more heat than butter. Fillets turn out beautifully brown and crispy.

Walleye fillets are an excellent protein complement to eggs for the breakfast menu.

BROILED WALLEYE

Walleye fillets or small whole walleyes (cleaned, with head and
    scales removed)
Bread or cracker crumbs or Shake 'n Bake, if desired
¼ cup melted butter, margarine, or oil
Salt, pepper, or other seasonings

Rinse fish in water or milk, shaking off excess moisture. If you
wish to bread the fillets, shake them in a bag with the crumbs.
Arrange fish on broiler pan; brush lightly with melted butter
(to which a little lemon juice may be added); season to taste.
Place under medium heat. Allow fish to brown, occasionally
brushing with butter. Large fillets and whole fish should be
turned once to make sure they cook through. Serve with tartar
sauce, catsup, and lemon wedges.

FRESH FILLET OF WALLEYE
WITH WILD RICE AND SAUCE AMANDINE

8 walleye fillets
Salt and pepper
Dried bread crumbs
6 ounces wild rice
¾ pound butter
6 ounces sliced almonds
Spiced peaches if desired

Preheat oven to 450 degrees. Season walleye fillets with salt
and pepper. Roll in dried bread crumbs. Bake fillets in oven for
15 minutes or until the fish begins to flake. Do not overcook.
To prepare wild rice: Wash rice thoroughly. Put rice in sauce-
pan with 4 cups of salted water; bring to a boil. Simmer covered
for 45 minutes until rice is tender but not mushy. Uncover and
simmer for an additional 5 minutes.

Just before serving, sauté almonds in butter. To serve, place
fillets on individual plates with wild rice on the side. Spoon
butter and almonds over the fillets and rice and garnish with
spiced peaches if desired. Serves 8.

WALLEYE FILLETS WITH WINE

½ teaspoon white pepper
1 teaspoon salt
1 teaspoon paprika
2 tablespoons flour
3 pounds walleye fillets
¼ pound butter
1 cup sour cream
1 cup white wine
Juice of ½ lemon
2 tablespoons minced parsley
2 tablespoons minced chives
½ teaspoon oregano
¼ teaspoon sweet basil

Mix pepper, salt, paprika, and flour and put mixture into a paper bag. Shake fillets in the bag, a few at a time, to coat with seasoned flour. Brown them slightly on both sides in the butter. Place fillets carefully in a casserole. Mix all the other ingredients together and pour over fish. Place in a 400-degree oven, uncovered, for 10 to 15 minutes. Serve with French bread or rolls for sopping up the sauce. Serves 6.

WALLEYE FONDUE

Walleye fillets (allow ¼ pound per person)
½ cup milk
1 egg
Cracker, bread, or corn flake crumbs, or cornmeal
Cooking oil
Fish sauces (such as tartar sauce and catsup)
Lemon wedges

Cut fillets into 1-inch cubes. Bread cubes by dipping them in milk-egg mixture and then into crumbs. Heat oil on stove ahead of time until hot, then put into fondue pot, so that fish cubes will brown quickly. Serve with fish sauces and lemon wedges.

BAKED STUFFED WALLEYE

Walleye (preferably over 4 pounds), cleaned, with head and
   dorsal fins removed
Stuffing:
   30 soda crackers
   1 small can oysters, undrained
   ½ cup milk
   Salt and pepper and sage
Bacon

Prepare stuffing by mixing crackers, oysters, and milk together
and seasoning to taste. Stuff belly cavity of fish; sew flaps
together. Place fish on rack in roaster. Arrange several bacon
strips on top of fish and wedge more bacon into groove where
fins were removed. Bake in a 250-degree oven for 2½ hours
(increase time for larger fish) or until fish is white and flaky.

(Erma Barneveld, Wealthwood, Minnesota)

WALLEYE CHOWDER

2 cups boneless walleye meat (preferably fillets), or more if
   desired
½ cup chopped celery, or more if desired
1 onion, chopped
Bacon strips
1 can cream of potato soup
1 can water, or 1½ cans milk
2 tablespoons butter
Pinch of parsley flakes
Salt, pepper, or other seasonings

Boil or steam walleye meat with celery and onion in a small
amount of water; drain when cooked through. Fry several bacon
strips until crisp; drain, then crumble into pieces. Combine all
ingredients; season to taste. Bring to boil, then simmer for
15-20 minutes or longer, stirring regularly. To make a thicker
chowder, add less liquid.

DEEP-FRIED WALLEYE CHEEKS

Walleye cheeks (preferably from walleyes over 2 pounds)
Cracker, bread, or corn flake crumbs, or cornmeal

Remove cheeks from walleyes and peel off skins. Coat cheeks with breading and fry in deep fryer until golden brown.

Walleye cheeks are a delicacy somewhat resembling scallops.

The classic shore lunch featuring fresh walleye fillets.

NOTES

Part 1: The Walleye

[1]Henry A. Regier, Richard A. Ryder, and Vernon Applegate, *The Ecology and Management of the Walleye in Western Lake Erie* (Ann Arbor: Great Lakes Fishery Commission, 1969), pp. 12-14. MacKay in *Fishes of Ontario* (Ontario Department of Land and Forests, 1963), lists New Brunswick as the northeasternmost point of walleye distribution in North America. Churchill, Niemuth, and Wirth (see footnote 3) include Labrador as part of the northeastern boundary of the walleye range. Libbey (see footnote 14) calls the northern limits of the walleye range "indefinite."

[2]These figures include the millions of fry, walleyes less than two inches long. Between four and six million fingerlings from two to six inches are part of the artificially propagated total in Minnesota.

[3]Warren Churchill, Wallace Niemuth, and Thomas Wirth, *The Walleye: Life History, Ecology, and Management,* Wisconsin Conservation Department Publication no. 222, 1959.

[4]Ibid.

[5]This color difference may be due to the presence of a special strain or subspecies of walleye. In order to retain their unique characteristics, members of a subgroup would have to spawn apart from the main group.

[6]The big sauger was caught by Mike Fischer of Chaseley, North Dakota, fishing on Douglas Bay of Lake Sakakawea, October 6, 1971.

[7]Regier, Ryder, and Applegate, p. 15.

[8]Kit Bergh, *Minnesota Fish and Fishing* (Minneapolis: T. S. Denison and Company, 1958), pp. 146-147.

[9]Kenneth D. Carlander and Robert E. Cleary, "The Daily Activity Patterns of Some Freshwater Fishes," *The American Midland Naturalist* XLI (March 1949), pp. 447-452.

[10]The Carlander and Cleary studies also produced the following information of interest to anglers: 1. Saugers seem to move

more during the day. 2. Perch are most active in daytime, more being caught in the nets in the afternoon than in the morning. 3. Northerns were taken in daylight hours. 4. The carp in Clear Lake were shallowest during the day. 5. Suckers roamed the shallows at night. 6. Bullheads moved shallower at night. (See page 19 of this book about "rest requirements" of walleyes and perch.)

[11]Regier, Ryder, and Applegate, p. 16.

[12]With most fish, food consumption and energy requirements vary with water temperature. More food and energy are required during the winter months.

See Karl F. Lagler, John E. Bardach, and Robert R. Miller, *Ichthyology: The Study of Fishes* (New York: John Wiley and Sons, Inc., 1962), pp. 172-178.

[13]Fritz H. Johnson, "Environmental and Species Associations of the Walleye in Lake Winnibigoshish and Connected Waters, Including Observations on Food Habits and Predator-Prey Relationships," *Minnesota's Fisheries Investigations*, no. 5 (June 1969). *Minnesota Fisheries Investigations* is an occasional publication of the Division of Game and Fish, 390 Centennial Office Building, St. Paul, Minnesota 55101.

[14]Jake Eldridge Libbey, "Certain Aspects of the Life History of the Walleye, Stizostedion Vitreum (Mitchell), in Dale Hollow Reservoir, Tennessee, Kentucky, with Emphasis on Spawning" (M. A. thesis, Tennessee Technological University, 1969.)

See also Kevin Allen Muench, "Certain Aspects of the Life History of the Walleye, Stizostedion Vitreum (Mitchell), in Center Hill Reservoir, Tennessee" (M.A. thesis, Tennessee Technological University, 1966).

[15]Churchill, Niemuth, and Wirth.

[16]B. Durbach, "The Adverse Effect of Cold Weather upon the Successful Reproduction of Pickerel, Stizostedion Vitreum Vitreum, at Heming Lake, Manitoba in 1947," *The Canadian Fish Culturist* II (December 1947), pp. 22-23.

[17]John D. O'Donnell, "The Walleyed Pike Run in Knutson Creek," Wisconsin Conservation Department Report, 1941.

In his study of the walleye spawning runs at Little Cutfoot Sioux, Fritz Johnson notes that the average starting date of the run is April 17, with a water temperature of 38°F. The duration of the run is extended by cold weather, shortened by warm temperatures.

See Fritz H. Johnson, *Numerical Abundance, Sex Ratios, and Size-Age Composition of the Walleye Spawning Run at Little Cutfoot Sioux Lake, Minnesota, 1942-1969, with Data on Fecundity and Incidence of Lymphocystis,* Investigational Report no. 315 (1971), p. 3, prepared for the Minnesota Department of Natural Resources, Division of Game and Fish, Section of Fisheries, St. Paul.

[18]In 1954, heavy winds during spawning time at Mille Lacs Lake piled eggs in windrows along the shoreline. Despite that egg loss, conservation officials estimate that 1954's crop of young walleyes in Mille Lacs was good.

See J. E. Maloney and F. H. Johnson, "Life Histories and Inter-Relationships of Walleye and Yellow Perch, Especially during Their First Summer, in Two Minnesota Lakes," *Transactions of the American Fisheries Society* LXXXV (1957), p. 192.

[19]Fritz H. Johnson, "Walleye Egg Survival during Incubation on Several Types of Bottom in Lake Winnibigoshish, Minnesota and Connecting Waters," *Transactions of the American Fisheries Society* XC (July 1961), pp. 312-322.

[20]During this period when the walleye fry are pelagic, inhabiting waters near the surface, the vertical depth of the fry varies from lake to lake. For example, Johnson found that in Little Cutfoot Sioux Lake where water is turbid, the fry concentrate at the surface. (See note 17.) In clearer lakes, such as Mille Lacs, the fry are distributed as far as ten feet below the surface, with a less pronounced tendency to concentrate at the surface.

[21]John Dobie, "Food and Feeding Habits of the Walleye, Stizostedion Vitreum Vitreum, and Associated Game and Forage Fishes in Lake Vermilion, Minnesota, with Special Reference to the Tullibee, Coregonus (Leucichthys) Artedi," *Minnesota Fisheries Investigations,* no. 4 (July 1966), pp. 39-71.

[22]J. E. Maloney and F. H. Johnson, pp. 197-198.

[23]Dennis Schupp, "New Knowledge about Walleyes: Research on Leech Lake," *Gopher Angler,* May-June 1970, pp. 2-5.

[24]Donald E. Olson, "Sex Ratios of Young-of-the-Year Walleyes

in Minnesota Rearing Ponds and Lakes," *The Progressive Fish-Culturist* XXX (October 1968), pp. 196-202.

[25]Fritz H. Johnson, *Survival of Stocked Walleye Fingerlings in Northern Minnesota Lakes as Estimated from the Age-Composition of Experimental Gill Net Catches,* Investigational Report no. 314 (1971), p. 7, prepared for the Minnesota Department of Natural Resources, Division of Game and Fish, Section of Research and Planning, St. Paul.

Johnson notes that "no significant increase in year-class abundance was found for natural walleye lakes as a result of fingerling stocking," although he believes that a series of several fingerling plants over six to eight years might increase the over-all walleye population of those lakes. Johnson says, "There is no evidence that the walleye populations of the stocked natural walleye lakes sampled were increased over that which might occur naturally without stocking." Thus, anglers' and sportsmen's groups would do better to concentrate on developing gravel-rubble spawning ground improvements on their lakes than to continually clamor for more stocking.

On the other hand, Johnson's study shows that present stocking rates on bass-panfish lakes studied are adequate to improve a year-class of walleyes, provided other factors influencing the survival of the fingerlings are favorable. Evidence suggests that stocked fingerlings of larger sizes have better survival potentials.

[26]Lloyd L. Smith and Richard L. Pycha, "Factors Related to Commercial Production of the Walleye in Red Lakes, Minnesota," *Transactions of the American Fisheries Society* XC (April 1961), pp. 190-217.

[27]Regier, Ryder, and Applegate, p. 24.

[28]*The Story of the Walleye,* Minnesota Conservation Bulletin no. 8, Bureau of Information, 350 Centennial Office Building, St. Paul, Minnesota 55101.

[29]The fish louse in question is *Argulus,* an external parasite. *Argulus* is dependent on the blood of the host fish. The lice congregate on the back of the fish directly behind the head, and sometimes cause a raw spot of an inch or more in diameter. *Argulus* can swim freely from one fish to another.

By themselves, the fish lice seldom cause mortality. However, if a walleye population is weakened by unusually high summer water temperatures, the added burden of an emergence of lice at that time could prove fatal for some fish.

[30]Roland Walker, "Warty Walleyes," *New York State Conservationist,* October-November 1957. *See also* Fritz Johnson's study, note 17.

[31]Churchill, Niemuth, and Wirth.

[32]The world's record walleye was taken by Mabry Harper on August 1, 1960, at Old Hickory Lake, Tennessee.

See also the interview with Gearhart Block and accompanying photo in Part 3 of this book. His ability and location combine to yield over forty ten-pounders nearly every fall.

Others have cashed in on big walleyes. In 1952, Blanche Baker broke the New York state record with a walleye weighing 15 pounds, 3 ounces, taken from the Chemung River in Chemung County. Harold "Curly" Lehn of Bemidji, Minnesota has two walleyes over 16 pounds to his credit, just shy of the Minnesota record.

Minnesota's Department of Natural Resources lists the following catches: 1. 16 pounds, 11 ounces by an unnamed angler at Basswood Lake, 1955. 2. 16 pounds, 8 ounces by John E. Nortelli of Finlayson at Sturgeon Lake, Pine County. 3. 16 pounds, 8 ounces by Mitch Redarcheck of Graceton at Lake of the Woods, 1959. 4. 16 pounds, 6 ounces by Harold Lehn of Bemidji at Lake Bemidji. 5. 16 pounds, 4 ounces by Martin Hammersmith of Elmhurst, Illinois, at Moose Lake near Ely, 1949. Walleyes over ten pounds are caught annually in nearly all areas where these fish are found.

Part 2: Walleye Fishing

[1]In discussing the pros and cons of rough and calm water for walleye fishing, it cannot be overemphasized that walleyes are sometimes more cooperative in calm water, contrary to the old sayings, especially in the deeper areas.

[2]On rare occasions, usually in summer when deep water may have reduced oxygen levels in certain lakes, walleyes cruise shallow weedy areas. Faced with the dilemma of deep water with little oxygen against clear and warm shallower water, the walleye might select the shallows, seeking weeds for protection from bright sunlight. There is very little chance of worthwhile concentrations, though.

[3]Occasionally small schools of walleyes may congregate around and in submerged brush piles. These are difficult to locate and hard to fish, yet their potential remains.

206

Al Reinfelder, *Bait Tail Fishing* (New York: A. S. Barnes & Company, Inc., 1969), p. 16.

[5]Attachment of a trailer hook sometimes solves the "short strike" problem. Some jig manufacturers handle a special line of jigs featuring small treble trailers. I use a trailer hook sparingly because I feel they discourage fish from striking; others disagree.

[6]Fatheads, suckers, and various kinds of shiners and chubs are commonly used throughout much of the walleye range. Wholesalers traffic minnows for hundreds of miles.

[7]Arthur H. Carhart, *Fresh Water Fishing* (New York: A. S. Barnes & Company, Inc., 1949), pp. 84-85.

[8]Merle W. Johnson, *A Five-year Study of the Sport Fishery of Mille Lacs Lake, Minnesota,* Investigational Report no. 273 (March 1964), prepared for the Minnesota Department of Natural Resources, Division of Game and Fish, Section of Research and Planning, St. Paul.

INDEX